A Practical Guide to

Data Communications Management

AUERBACH Data Processing Management Library

James Hannan, Editor

•

Contributors To This Volume

James W. Conard
Conard Associates, Costa Mesa CA

———

Pete Moulton
Columbia MD

———

Thomas J. Murray
SUNGARD Technical Consultant, Sun Information Services Company
Philadelphia PA

———

Richard Parkinson
Senior Consultant, Consultec Canada Limited, Vancouver BC

———

Joseph St. Amand
QED Information Services, Wellesley MA

———

Mark Strangio
Communications Analyst, Codex Corporation, Mansfield MA

———

Dr. Rein Turn
Professor, California State University, Northbridge CA

———

Gary Zielke
Director of Data Communications Management, Consultec Canada Limited
Vancouver BC

———

A Practical Guide to

Data Communications Management

Edited by James Hannan

AUERBACH Publishers Inc
Pennsauken NJ

VAN NOSTRAND REINHOLD COMPANY
New York Cincinnati Toronto London Melbourne

Copyright © 1982 by AUERBACH Publishers Inc

Library of Congress Catalog Card Number 82-11335

ISBN 0-442-20918-5

Printed in the United States of America

Published in the United States in 1982
by Van Nostrand Reinhold Company Inc
135 West 50th Street
New York NY 10020 USA

16 15 14 13 12 11 10 9 8 7 6 5 4 3 2

Library of Congress Cataloging in Publication Data
    Main entry under title:

    A Practical guide to data communications management.

      (Auerbach data processing management library ; v. 3)
      1. Data transmission systems.   2. Computer networks.
    I. Hannan, James, 1946-   . II. Series.
    TK5105.P7   1982   001.64'404   82-11335
    ISBN 0-442-20918-5 (Van Nostrand Reinhold Co. : pbk.)

Contents

Preface

In its relatively brief existence, the computer has emerged from the back rooms of most organizations to become an integral part of business life. Increasingly sophisticated data processing systems are being used today to solve increasingly complex business problems. As a result, the typical data processing function has become as intricate and specialized as the business enterprise it serves.

Such specialization places a strenuous burden on computer professionals. Not only must they possess specific technical expertise, they must understand how to apply their special knowledge in support of business objectives and goals. A computer professional's effectiveness and career hinge on how ably he or she manages this challenge.

To assist computer professionals in meeting this challenge, AUERBACH Publishers has developed the *AUERBACH Data Processing Management Library*. The series comprises eight volumes, each addressing the management of a specific DP function:

A Practical Guide to Data Processing Management
A Practical Guide to Programming Management
A Practical Guide to Data Communications Management
A Practical Guide to Data Base Management
A Practical Guide to Systems Development Management
A Practical Guide to Data Center Operations Management
A Practical Guide to EDP Auditing
A Practical Guide to Distributed Processing Management

Each volume contains well-tested, practical solutions to the most common and pressing set of problems facing the manager of that function. Supplying the solutions is a prominent group of DP practitioners—people who make their living in the areas they write about. The concise, focused chapters are designed to help the reader directly apply the solutions they contain to his or her environment.

AUERBACH has been serving the information needs of computer professionals for more than 25 years and knows how to help them increase their effectiveness and enhance their careers. The *AUERBACH Data Processing Management Library* is just one of the company's many offerings in this field.

James Hannan
Assistant Vice President
AUERBACH Publishers

Introduction

The astonishing advances in transportation and communications technology during the past several decades have made the world smaller and its resources more accessible. New patterns of social and business intercourse have consequently emerged to create what one analyst has termed a "global village." Within the confines of that village businesses and governments have intensified their competition for a share of the world's markets. In such an atmosphere, decisions must be made expeditiously—even though the complexity and location of decision-making information often render the process difficult. As a consequence, the need to locate and transmit accurate and timely information has become more urgent.

The growing importance of communications in the conduct of business and governmental affairs has increased the visibility of the data communications function. This presents data communications managers with both an opportunity and a challenge. They have the opportunity to make a substantive contribution to their organizations' strategic planning and decision making. But in order to do so, they must understand and harness the rapidly changing communications technology as well as apply proven management and planning techniques to their operations. This volume of the *AUERBACH Data Processing Management Library* is designed to help data communications managers meet that challenge.

We have commissioned an outstanding group of communications practitioners to share the benefits of their extensive and varied experience. Our authors have written on a carefully chosen range of topics and have provided proven, practical advice for managing the data communications function productively.

In Chapter One, Mark Strangio discusses the trends in communications technology that the data comm manager must be aware of to plan effectively and make informed decisions. He treats such areas as data communications equipment, transmission facilities, network management and control, and the distribution of information and communications capabilities to remote sites.

A much-discussed trend in recent years is that toward all-digital communications. Although some skeptics might argue that this trend is more apparent than real, the shrewd data comm manager should at least understand the technology and what is and will be possible. In "Perspective on Digital Communications," Richard Parkinson discusses the background, current status, and future of the telecommunications industry.

Introduction

While knowledge of industry and technology trends can help data comm managers in long-range planning, they need additional tools for operational-level planning. A key operational issue is network planning and design. In formulating network requirements, data comm managers cannot rely solely on the projected data transmission loads of the network sites because implementation status and applications priorities change. To accommodate these changes, Pete Moulton presents in Chapter Three a methodology for formulating network requirements and provides cataloging forms that can be used in the process.

Another important operational-level planning issue is choosing communications standards. Improperly applying standards or ignoring their impact can lead to chaotic compatibility problems. In Chapter Four, James W. Conard focuses on the application of protocol standards and offers practical advice on selecting standards. In Chapter Five, Richard Parkinson describes one of the newer standards—RS-449. He discusses the standard's evolution, functions, and capabilities (as well as those of its companion standards, RS-422 and RS-423) and draws appropriate parallels to RS-232C.

A network architecture that has become a de facto standard since its introduction in the mid-1970s is IBM's System Network Architecture (SNA). SNA comprises both hardware and software components and provides a common approach for centralized as well as decentralized applications. In Chapter Six, Pete Moulton provides a sound fundamental understanding of SNA product offerings. In Chapter Seven, Joseph St. Amand discusses SNA-like architectures and capabilities and suggests ways to achieve SNA functionality with non-IBM hardware and software.

Because so many organizations have become vitally dependent on their data communications networks, it is incumbent on data comm managers to address such crucial issues as data security, network reliability and availability, and disaster recovery. In "Encryption for Data Security," Dr. Rein Turn provides an introduction to the purposes, principles, and applications of cryptography in data security. Gary Zielke discusses network control systems that can aid the manager in maintaining a high degree of network availability and reliability in Chapter Nine. And in Chapter Ten, Thomas J. Murray examines network disaster planning, detailing the steps and strategies required to implement and maintain a disaster recovery plan.

1 Trends in Data Communications Technology

by Mark Strangio

INTRODUCTION

As communications technologies become increasingly important to the success of many organizations, gains in productivity that can be attributed to the new technologies will, in turn, fuel the demand for further improvements. A number of potential gains can be identified:

- Decreased costs for DP and communications hardware
- Improved intra- and intercorporate communications through electronic mail/message systems, teleconferencing, and digital facsimile systems
- The elimination of redundant or time-consuming tasks through communicating/distributed WP systems
- The reduction of voice network costs through speech-digitizing technologies
- Improved man-machine interfaces through distributed graphics and color terminals
- Improved record storage, retrieval, and integrity through distributed data base systems
- Improved circuit efficiencies through data traffic management, circuit switching, and resource selection systems

This chapter examines the technological advances that will make these gains possible and discusses trends in technology and vendor offerings as well as major issues of concern to the data communications manager. No attempt is made to quantify, however, or to predict when or to what degree changes may occur.

BACKGROUND

The major determinant of data network architectures has historically been the implementation of data communications equipment (e.g., multiplexors) and transmission facilities that improve circuit performance and efficiencies. In addition, regulatory changes, begun in the late 1960s, are positively affecting the telecommunications industry and opening new markets to competition.

In the area of private data networks, the introduction of time division multiplexors and, more recently, statistical multiplexors has greatly improved the bit-per-dollar transportation ratios associated with multiple remote terminals. In essence, the multiplexor has eliminated the individualized circuits over which frequently inactive terminals communicated with a centralized host processor. Additional multiplexor-based innovations (e.g., data compression, sophisticated error protection schemes, and network/traffic analysis features) have further enhanced circuit efficiencies and control capabilities.

The evolution of efficient front-end-based communications protocols (from simplex to bisynchronous to truly full-duplex bit-oriented protocols) has improved the performance of multipoint configurations. These protocols have decreased the response time and, in turn, permitted expansion of the multipoint circuit in terms of the number of drops or devices per circuit.

Both domestic and international public data networks have similarly realized greater efficiencies by introducing packet-switching technologies. The X.25 standard, for example, allows multiple users to share high-speed transmission facilities that would otherwise be prohibitively expensive (given the low volume of an individual user's traffic). One key to the continued success of X.25 public data networks will be the ease with which private (non-X.25) networks can be interfaced with the public networks. A primary benefit here is that as public data networks proliferate and become increasingly standardized, thereby permitting easy access, they will complement rather than replace the private data network, facilitating both intra- and intercorporate communications.

At the present time, the conventional data communications network consists of modems, multiplexors, concentrators, front-end processors, data-matrix switches, monitoring/control/management equipment, and various leased and switched terrestrial and satellite transmission facilities. These components are organized into combinations of point-to-point, multipoint, star, and delta topologies. Connected to this network are central processing units, peripheral storage devices, cluster controllers, Teletype-equivalent terminals, intelligent terminals, and other miscellaneous ancillary devices. The intricacies of interdevice and intra-/internetwork communications are handled using combinations of standard hardware interfaces, software protocols, and specialized network control applications packages.

Several significant technological innovations will increasingly affect conventional data communications network topologies and network component integration: the proliferation of distributed DP, the integration of non-DP functions within the data communications network, and the incorporation of application-independent teleprocessing and resource-sharing/switching systems. The trend toward distributed DP capabilities is propelled, typically, by a number of key factors, including the need to:

- Enhance overall network reliability—This will be realized by eliminating the possibility of total system failure if central-site host(s) or front-end processors fail.

- Optimize and/or preserve the host's performance—DDP, accompanied by careful data base management and the high connectivity of central and remote processors (through software and hardware standardization), should diminish central site degradation and enhancement costs.
- Implement high-performance technologies—Intelligent terminals, controllers, and minicomputers with previously unattainable price/ performance ratios will continue to create savings through gains in productivity and decreases in communications costs. Ultimately, the organization's DP communications managers and users will seek to distribute computation and data base resources closest to those areas where the work is performed or the information needed. In the area of circuit performance, the data communications network manager will seek to:
  —Eliminate from the circuit all data and data control bits that are not crucial to the transportation of information
  —Eliminate idle circuit time or space by packing the circuit with useful information, optimizing network design, and implementing efficient network/circuit/link control software (e.g., HDLC)

Network Topologies and Component Integration

The effects of these forces upon the network topology will be measured, for example, in terms of the proliferation of high-speed backbone circuits that support interprocessor communications. Increasingly, the conventional network will consist of a mainframe, multiple mainframes at a central site, or multiple mainframes at multiple sites. These processors will support multiple distributed minicomputer systems that, in turn, support multitiered (second-, third-, and fourth-level), multiplexed, point-to-point, and multipoint circuits. It will be necessary to ensure that hardware and software are relatively compatible and that compatibility exists with integrated subsystems whose purpose is, for example, to observe or to monitor, control, and manage the network. As networks become more complex in distributed DP, such subsystems must be capable of being extended to or through all components and levels of the network. For larger networks, multiple points can facilitate efficient network operation. The subsystem must also be able to provide a high degree of functionality while remaining transparent and nondisruptive to the primary network function: data and information transportation. Other factors that will influence network architectures include:

- The integration of new systems and technologies, such as electronic mail/message switching (EMS) or digital facsimile transmission with DP networks
- The integration of previously nondigital communications systems or functions (e.g., voice)

To the greatest extent possible, network managers will seek to incorporate new systems such as EMS within the existing data network. For example, an organization may want to provide EMS to a remote site that already has an interactive interface to a central site for accounting or order entry. Rather than add a dedicated lower-speed circuit to the remote site, it would be desirable to provide time slots for EMS by statistically multiplexing the existing circuit. This may be especially preferable where interactive and low-utilization single-purpose terminals predominate at the remote site. Alternatively, for the remote site that accommodates fewer terminals or serves as the hub of lower-level or tail circuits, it would be appropriate to dedicate frequency slots for EMS by using multiplexor modems. These are ideal for providing multiple application-independent channels where the aggregate traffic does not exceed the limits of a 3002 voicegrade channel (a total of 9,600 bits per second).

Integrating Voice and Data

An average corporation must currently maintain at least two separate communications networks: one or more for data and one for voice. As pressures mount for greater efficiency in both kinds of networks, the demand to add at least some voice traffic to the data network will increase. Voice (which is analog) is transmitted over the 3,000 Hz bandwidth of the voicegrade telephone circuit. Historically, combining analog and digital traffic has been technically and administratively difficult. One solution, however, is to digitize the voice at a sufficiently low data rate (preferably 2,400 bits per second), allowing the digitized voice traffic to be treated like any other data stream in the data network. Given the demand for this capability, therefore, it is likely that the following trends will become increasingly important:

- Speech-digitizing technology for transmission at 2,400 bits per second will improve in quality, reliability, and flexibility such that digitized voice traffic will represent a greater percentage of the total data network traffic.
- Digitized voice traffic will be integrated by allocating time slots to voice-digitizing terminals through statistical multiplexing.
- The ability to share these terminals among specified corporate users and switch the digitized voice traffic over the data network to compatible remote sites will become common as interfaces to computerized private branch exchanges evolve.
- Packetizing digital voice traffic for transmission over X.25 networks will facilitate the acceptance and use of voice-digitizing technologies.
- The ability to encrypt digital voice traffic will facilitate the use of voice digitizing in organizations requiring secure voice communications.

An alternative to digitizing voice traffic is replacing the telephone plant with all-digital high-speed transmission facilities. Computer data would be handled in its native form, and voice traffic would be converted to high-speed digital format (64K bits per second), preserving speech quality. This is an attractive technical approach, particularly in terms of the need for higher-speed communications (more than 9,600 bits per second) between computers and terminals, a limitation imposed by the analog telephone plant. The difficulty with this approach, however, is economic rather than technical. The billions of dollars invested in the millions of miles of conventional analog facilities preclude their replacement in the near future. Even though some all-digital long-haul facilities (e.g., Bell's DDS) have been and continue to be implemented in the U.S., there is virtually no local digital distribution system between the subscriber and the central telephone office. Alternative solutions, such as the use of optical fibers or bypassing underground cable systems with satellite and microwave facilities, will be implemented. Cost factors, however, will confine these alternatives to backbone/high-speed networks and, in general, very large scale networks.

Data Communications Hardware and Software

The evolution of data communications hardware and software will primarily focus on modulation products (modems), network technologies (advanced statistical multiplexing, concentration, and circuit switching), carrier systems, and network management and control systems. It should be noted that developments in each of these areas are affected significantly by advances in component technology and software development.

The trend in component technology (e.g., LSI and VLSI components) has been toward markedly decreasing unit costs. Because of the great demand, low supply, and high manufacturing costs associated with advanced microprocessor chips (e.g., the 16-bit microprocessor), however, it is likely that there will be a diminution in the rate at which hardware costs decline. Similarly, the demand for modifiable software will drive up development costs and exacerbate development problems. If this trend offers any advantage to the user, it will be in the degree to which standardized software will be used and software documentation made available.

Modulation Products

Technological changes and/or trends in modulation products are likely to be implemented in several ways, as is discussed in the following paragraphs. The essential criterion to the user will be device reliability.

- High-, medium-, and low-speed and short-haul modems will increasingly be integrated with, and central to, network monitoring, testing, and control functions. Device functionality in monitoring and testing analog and digital parameters and interfaces will become paramount to the network operator. Device and circuit backup and restoration from a central control point will be essential for most networks in which component failure is synonymous with large revenue losses.
- Improvements in high-speed modem performance (e.g., transmission at speeds greater than 9,600 bits per second over voicegrade lines) will be modest. Modulation schemes for greater speeds will be inordinately complex and expensive; moreover, problems associated with circuit quality and retransmission/error correction may diminish the cost/ performance benefits.
- Multipoint modems operating at speeds of 9,600 bits per second outbound and inbound with low training/turnaround times (e.g., 20 to 35 milliseconds) will become available. The predominant multipoint ap-

plication, however, will be one in which inbound transmissions are short; circuit performance and response times will be optimized by lower-cost devices that provide lower inbound speeds with short turn-around times.

- Dial modems with automatic fallback to lower bit transmission and audio signaling rates will enhance operation at 9,600 bits per second.
- Two-wire full-duplex modems operating at speeds from 1,200 to 4,800 bits per second will become increasingly popular for use in switched networks.
- Modems that use a secondary or sideband channel(s) to transmit network control and telemetry information will have the continued advantage of operator functionality without imposing overhead on, or interfering with, the primary channel.
- High-speed modems with built-in smart multiplexors, automatic retransmission of (erroneous) data, encryption, and other optional features are likely to appear.
- Most modem manufacturers will use a combination of custom LSI and VLSI and microprocessor technologies, resulting in devices that are more expensive to develop, less expensive to manufacture, simpler to modify, and capable of implementing more sophisticated algorithms and operating modes.
- Programmability in modems will permit the accumulation of application-specific as well as standard data related to device and facility (e.g., circuit) performance and utilization.

Network Management and Control

Network management and control is (and will continue to be) one of the most interesting and complex issues confronting the data communications manager. Unlike various multiplexing technologies, there are tremendous functional differences among the various vendors' network control technologies. There are also radically disparate philosophies as to the purpose, residence (external or internal to the host), and responsibility of network management and control. Basically, the field of network control can be divided into two spheres. In one, network control and management resides within the host (as software); communications with network devices (modems) is accomplished by embedding or interleaving control data within the primary channel data frame. This protocol-based/protocol-sensitive approach allows a simpler modem design at the expense of some host-processor and circuit overhead. In the other approach, a network control and management system is a dedicated system, external to the host; communications with network devices is accomplished through a frequency-division multiplexed sideband or a secondary channel. The limited bandwidth of the secondary channel results in slower communications between the controller and modems; however, these systems are transparent to the primary channel protocol and do not add overhead to the host or circuit. They are also resistant to some forms of primary channel degradation.

The following changes or trends are likely to occur in the field of network management and control:

- Intelligence will continue to be distributed to network devices and will serve the control and management function. Modems, terminals, multiplexors, and nodal processors will fall within the domain of this function.
- Capabilities for surveillance or monitoring of digital and analog parameters will become more sophisticated, leading to faster identification and resolution of component malfunctions.
- All network components will be evaluated in terms of their ability to complement the control and management function.
- Remote switching and backup capabilities will become common in point-to-point as well as multipoint and multitiered configurations.
- Equipment and circuit performance data, derived from the control and management system, will become more central to the design and planning process.
- Greater emphasis will be placed upon simplifying the operator interface.

Network Products

Network products or technologies are commonly defined as systems that package and compress data/information units, perform and manage data link/circuit routing, provide protocol conversion and/or an effective interface between processing systems and varied transmission facilities, and provide circuit, terminal, and resource selection and switching.

The demand for advanced statistical multiplexing, concentrating, and circuit switching and nodal processors will continue to increase in both private and public data networks, and these technologies will continue to evolve. Optimum network performance may be achieved by implementing systems (using multiplexors or nodal processors) that are transparent to the application, enabling greater numbers of diverse applications to share the same network facilities. Some users, however, may prefer a concentrator-based network or multiple networks because of the efficiencies associated with applications to which the network systems/facilities are dedicated. The objectives for the network manager may include:

- Improved performance by increased data throughput and line utilization and by distributing data bases, thus lowering data file access times
- Improved management analysis features, such as line utilization statistics and error retransmission reports
- Minimizing growth costs by procuring modular equipment that is capable of growth
- Minimizing downtime costs and lowering productivity by procuring reliable systems that provide backup or redundant capabilities

The major trends associated with network technologies can be briefly summarized as follows:

- Private data networks will continue to proliferate, becoming more complex and using statistical multiplexing, concentration, and circuit-switching technologies. There will be an increasing demand to interface the private and public data networks, which will be accomplished through the development of firmware- and software-based network gateways.

- As processing/computation power and information storage and retrieval capabilities are distributed to remote sites, users and network operators will become increasingly aware of the benefits of terminal-to-terminal communications, such as electronic message switching or teleconferencing. This will be incorporated most efficiently by adding circuit-switching technologies that are independent of the DP function or equipment. This trend will be accompanied by, or be a result of, the transition from dumb to intelligent multifunctional terminals. With systems that provide hard-copy and online storage capabilities, benefits will typically include improved intracorporate communications, enhanced problem-solving capabilities, and faster information dissemination.
- Network-oriented hardware and software components will be developed to accommodate office functions and applications (e.g., WP, facsimile, electronic mail, and message switching). The implication is that the circuit-switching technologies themselves must be capable of disassembling and preassembling data units (e.g., packets, frames, blocks) created by many dissimilar terminals, while preserving protocol integrity. The protocol conversion function, therefore, will become embedded within circuit-switching equipment.
- Public data networks based on packet-switching X.25 technologies will continue to grow in Europe and will become far more common in North America.
- Voice and data network managers will seek to accommodate voice traffic in the digital networks. Multiplexing and circuit-switching technologies will incorporate voice-digitizing capabilities or, at a minimum, provide an effective interface to voice traffic. Voice message switching may emerge as a key value-added feature of public data networks.
- Network and data security will become increasingly important. Network technologies that accommodate the transmission of telemetry data (e.g., through the secondary channels) and/or encrypted data will be in high demand in such industries as banking.
- Network technologies will increasingly require remote/central-site access for control purposes and will, therefore, become more integrated with network management and control equipment.
- Redundancy and backup switching capabilities will become increasingly important at sites where equipment failure can be catastrophic.

VENDOR TRENDS

During the next 10 years, the data communications field will experience a rapid growth rate as well as an intensification of competitive forces within the marketplace. Over the long term, these forces will have a significant impact on the independent data communications equipment vendors and carriers as well as on mainframe, minicomputer, and office equipment manufacturers, whose systems will become increasingly linked to communications. Data communications equipment and services suppliers will be affected in a number of areas.

Structure and Orientation. The growth in number, size, and complexity of integrated multifunctional networks, coupled with the increasing ability of vendors to supply such networks, will increase vendor responsiveness to present as well as potential customers. Vendors will, for example, be called upon to provide such consulting services as product or network design and planning studies that are specific to the customer's network requirements. The vendor's organizational structure will increasingly be geared toward providing timely technical and management solutions to unique networking specifications. The vendor's market research staff and function will become more crucial in assessing trends in order to optimize the degree to which products and families of products will evolve and/or remain functional, upgradable, and enhanceable over extended periods.

It is also expected that data communications professionals will need to become more knowledgeable about DP hardware and software as well as the technologies that traditionally were not within their domain. Such knowledge should include distributed data base technologies, communicating word processors, integrated digital voice and data switching systems, and so on. Similarly, DP manufacturers will be under increasing pressure to understand and orient their products toward sophisticated communications technologies.

Research and Development. In order to meet the needs of broadened network/systems requirements and their concomitant technical complexities, vendor R&D departments will require larger development teams. These teams will be charged with the responsibilities of enforcing design-to-cost and designed-in-reliability development disciplines, providing total data communications systems solutions and ensuring technical/functional synergy between individual products, developing products to meet both domestic and international standards and specifications, providing capabilities for future enhancements, building serviceability into the product(s) via improved design and manufacturing techniques, and doing all of these while incorporating and gaining competence in leading-edge VLSI and microprocessor technologies. It must be emphasized that efficient software development will be increasingly critical to the success or failure of data communications products.

System Customization and Engineering. Again as a function of the increasing complexity of most users' data networks, each network will tend to become unique to the extent that system and/or component specifications will exceed those of standard products. It will therefore become critical for the vendor to retain technically outstanding and creative individuals in both the engineering and marketing departments. These resources will, in turn, be made available to the customer for building, designing, implementing, integrating, and supporting customized data communications subsystems. This position, as a primary customer interface, will be ideal for providing feedback on emerging customer requirements to R&D and corporate planning groups and will ensure development efforts that are responsive to market requirements and trends.

International and Domestic Distribution and Field Service. A discernible trend associated with user network growth is the evolution from national to international networks and/or more frequent interfaces with foreign or international networks. The effects upon the vendor are quite clear: the appropriate steps must be taken in product development to ensure that both domestic and international specifications are met; distribution and field service agreements must be developed for each country in which the vendor wishes to conduct business. Vendors must also ensure that foreign distributors and maintenance personnel are reliable, adequately supplied with parts, and sufficiently trained in operation, diagnostics, maintenance, and, in some cases, field repair of the products.

It should be obvious that the same criteria apply to vendors who choose third-party distribution, installation, and maintenance agreements for domestic operations. It is important to note here that users may occasionally evaluate a vendor's ability to service products solely on the number of field service locations—a somewhat restrictive criterion. Problems for the user (and the vendor) may arise because the third party is not sufficiently committed to the product, and direct service personnel inevitably receive better information and training.

Component/System Design. The demand for data communications components and complete systems from users with unique networking requirements and problems will underscore the need for vendors to adopt a holistic approach to product/systems planning and development. In the case of network products such as statistical multiplexors, vendors must ensure that a unit is cost-effective for the widest possible range of applications and can be upgraded to meet growing network requirements (e.g., number of terminals, traffic, throughput). Modular design will assuage user apprehensions of frequent large-capital outlays. Vendors will benefit by incurring fewer development projects and costs, greater manufacturing efficiencies, fewer (and less frequent) upgrade issues to resolve, and lower recycling and refurbishing costs.

Complexity

Because of the growing complexity of data networks, users may prefer to deal with vendors who can provide the broadest range of solutions, equipment, and systems. A single-vendor approach to data communications requirements will facilitate the user's ability to isolate malfunctions or component degradations and take corrective action. It is safe to assume, therefore, that vendors will attempt (or be forced) to cover the spectrum of data communications components and ensure connectivity of the entire product line. The domain of the network management and control system, for example, will eventually be expanded to include multiplexors, front-end/nodal communications processors, data-switching systems, and terminals. More specifically, including the network/nodal processor requires that interpretive capabilities exist within the device, hardware/firmware/software-based interfaces exist, and the network/nodal processor and the management and control system be able to communicate over primary and/or secondary channels.

Software Complexity. Costs for hardware and software development programs have exhibited and will continue to exhibit dissimilar, if not opposite, behaviors. Hardware development and procurement costs tend to decelerate. Traditionally, this has been attributed to enhanced manufacturing processes, greater competition, increased or surplus supplies (e.g., 8-bit microprocessors), or the fact that much hardware cannot be altered. Software, on the other hand, is the perfect candidate for alteration. Software is never complete, it is never entirely debugged, it is inevitably not as efficient as originally intended—and its development is very difficult to contain. In order to manage software development programs more effectively, vendors will be forced to:
- Provide time-saving development tools
- Improve documentation practices
- Improve program definition and specification

ISSUES OF CONCERN TO THE DATA COMMUNICATIONS MANAGER

Although this chapter deals with trends in the various data communications technologies, there are issues relating to the management of networks, the technical expertise of personnel, and the like that are of great concern to the data communications manager. These issues can become a major determinant of the daily information transportation operations.

The Manager's Function and Responsibilities

The data communications manager will be under increased pressure to learn more about new and existing technologies. Technological innovations that facilitate the integration of data and voice communications systems may profoundly affect the corporate management structure. Placing responsibility for a portion of the voice network function within the domain of the data communications manager may therefore limit the introduction of cost-saving technologies. Especially in cases involving reorganization, the data communications manager will be forced to present a very strong argument regarding the technical and management efficiencies of implementing the innovation. This implies not only that the manager must be proficient in virtually all aspects of the innovation before implementation but that he or she must assume responsibility for its success or failure. The fact is that innovations in voice communications, data communications, and DP tend to inhibit the differentiation of management responsibilities and functions.

Another problem will be the continued or increasing shortage of professionals who have technical and administrative expertise in communications systems, who understand the implications of an integrated system, and who can develop creative solutions that will lead the organization along the best path. This shortage is directly related to the lack of communications courses and programs in higher and technical educational institutions. As a result, many managers will be forced to hire entry-level people, provide them with in-house training programs, and/or subsidize external seminars. The data communications manager will also be faced with other training-related problems, including:

- The accumulation of technical information from publications and consultants
- Obtaining information on existing, new, and future products and objectives from vendors
- Translating and disseminating to nontechnical user groups information pertaining to the function, operation, and, in some cases, maintenance of existing equipment as well as new systems as they are integrated

Further complicating the manager's life will be the responsibility for all of these problems while responding effectively to the daily network problems that inevitably occur in a crisis-driven environment. It must be emphasized that the manager is (and will continue to be) the person responsible should the network fail. Businesses that depend on a real-time data communications network will increasingly measure the cost of network downtime in terms of lost revenue.

The Increasing Complexity of Networks

It is possible to define greater network complexity in terms of more circuits, greater numbers of more diverse types of terminals, and the integration of more intelligent remote communications network processors. Network components must be able to accommodate circuit or terminal growth. The addition of circuits and terminals that interface with a network processor usually results in increased traffic and, in turn, demands more of the network processor's throughput and buffering capabilities. The addition of processor modules is a preferred solution when evaluating such costly and disruptive alternatives as adding a smaller device, replacing the device with one that is bigger, adding another (redundant) network, or restricting the growth of the network and (in turn) the organization's business functions.

Greater network or terminal functionality will require that communications processors be capable of handling diversity by allowing simple firmware or software (protocol-based) additions, options, or enhancements. For example, the change to HDLC protocols and the addition of integrated multiplexing or circuit-switching systems require incorporation of asynchronous, bisynchronous, and full-duplex capabilities. Systems that can downline-load software revisions to unattended remote communications processors will be preferred.

The growth in X.25-based public data networks will increase the demand for interfaces that permit cost-effective communications between private and public networks. For example, the use of a public data network facility to add on a remote low-traffic terminal may be preferred to dial-up or leased facilities. Network processors or concentrators must, therefore, be capable of adding a packet assembly-disassembly module.

Increased network complexity translates directly into greater dissimilarities in network topologies, components, and applications. The data communications manager will attempt to optimize network performance, operation, expandability, and functionality, while maximizing the use of standard modular equipment and minimizing costly special development or customization projects. The manager will have to deal with such considerations as:

- Backup or redundant transmission facilities for large multipoint and multiprocessor networks and networks that use high-speed, wideband, or digital backbone circuits
- Sharing and switching facilities to backup host and front-end processors
- Extended network control through concentrator/distributed processor sites to lower-level/tail circuits
- Integrated networks using DP and communications equipment from multiple vendors

The demand to incorporate technological innovations will make the network more complex from both a technical and a management perspective, as follows:

- Voice-digitizing technologies—These will increase the demand to transport voice traffic over the data network. High-quality speech-digitizing technologies at a low bit rate will allow the transmission of several separate voice conversations over a single circuit. The growth of the data network's transmission facilities and circuit-switching capabilities will accelerate. Digitizing technologies may be integrated with a digital CBX or be implemented in separate systems or terminals that can be interfaced with the CBX.
- Encryption and network security devices—The need to encrypt both data and digitized voice traffic will increase. Encryption mechanisms will be capable of single-channel as well as bulk encryption. Such industries as banking will require the capability to transmit telemetry data along with primary channel and network control data.
- Integrated voice/data digital switching systems—Mechanisms that can perform the circuit/link-switching function for both voice and data networks will become available.
- Communicating WP and electronic mail systems—There will be an increased demand to distribute WP and electronic mail capabilities to remote sites. Remote sites already connected to the data network for DP will attempt to integrate these diverse functions. The result will be an increased demand for more bandwidth, greater transmission speeds,

and nodal processors with circuit-switching, resource selection, and protocol conversion capabilities.

- Intelligent multifunctional terminals—As terminals become more intelligent and multifunctional, they will tend to become self-contained data/word processing, mail/message, and graphics systems. Terminal-system architectures will support various terminal protocols (2780/3780/HASP, 3270, TWX, telex, Teletex, X.25).

- Local distribution systems—Many organizations are currently confronted with the problem of providing low-, medium-, and high-speed transmission facilities in large complexes and buildings. While limited-distance modems or line drivers do provide and will continue to provide a cost-effective solution to this problem, the network manager will become involved with planning for fiber optic, digital microwave, and satellite and radio systems. Ideally, input for communications requirements should be solicited in the planning process for new buildings; it is much less expensive to install cable properly during construction.

Network Control and Management

It can be assumed that many organizations will become more dependent upon their integrated communications networks for successful business operations. It will therefore be incumbent upon the network manager to plan the growth of the network so as to optimize the integration of management and control systems. This task will be complicated by the greater number of choices in DP, transmission facility, and data communications equipment. As previously stated, a greater portion of a network's components will be brought within the network management and control system. With respect to the elements that have traditionally served this application (modems and the network controller), the network control function could be incorporated by upgrading or replacing PC boards with compatible modular-design modems and adding either an external-to-the-host hardware and software system or internal-to-the-host software. Increasingly, however, switching systems, multiplexors, nodal processors, and terminals will have optional management and control features, such as circuit traffic statistics, that necessitate communications with the network controller by way of the modems. All these elements must be designed to allow addition of the enabling components at the lowest possible cost.

It is important to note the distinction between the related concepts of network control and network management. Network control is primarily concerned with real-time monitoring, by either human operator or computer, of ongoing network operations and reacting to adverse conditions that disrupt operation. For instance, a network control site controller indicates that a remote terminal is streaming or that the bit error rate of a specified data circuit has exceeded a predefined threshold. The network operator would initiate diagnostic and testing procedures to isolate the cause and invoke commands to eliminate or bypass the failed or failing component. The operator might send a control message to the remote modem associated with the streaming terminal, with an instruction to disconnect the malfunctioning terminal from the line, thereby restoring the line for other devices. In the case of the excessive bit error rate, the operator would first execute a series of remote diagnostic loop tests (outbound, inbound, end to end) to isolate the problem and, subsequently, effect corrective action, such as:

- Substituting a dial-up link for a malfunctioning circuit
- Instructing modems to fall back to lower data transmission and audio signaling rates
- Remotely switching in a spare modem

Network management, on the other hand, is more forward looking and is concerned with such issues as cost and application effectiveness of the network; the need for network expansion; overall network reliability and availability; the effect of the data communications investment on profitability, productivity, or costs; and the utilization patterns of various corporate departments. The primary activity of network management systems is the collection of data generated in the network and the processing of that data to yield information that is useful to management. This information can then be used to support decisions concerning the data communications investment and corporate information flow in general. The system might, for example, capture data related to terminal utilization, including resources (host, application, data base) accessed by terminal and by user, average session duration, and so on. This data could be processed and analyzed to help management deal with such issues as allocation of terminal resources by department, allocation of DP overhead costs by department, and determining which data files to distribute to remote processors for planned DDP networks.

In selecting a network management and control system as well as the components and/or subsystems integral to the system, the network manager must ensure that the following features exist or can be incorporated as requirements or technologies evolve:

- Monitoring—the ability to observe or listen to the critical components of the network and to report degradations or failures as they occur. This function will increasingly include the monitoring of terminal, circuit, processor, and data base/file utilization.
- Testing/diagnostics—the ability to invoke procedures to isolate degrading or failed components.
- Control/restoration—the ability to effect corrective action.
- Management/reporting—the ability to process monitoring, testing/ diagnostic, and control/restoration data.

CONCLUSION

This chapter has discussed trends in data communications technologies, their effects on the organization, and their implications for the data communications manager. To deal with these changes and trends, it is essential that the DC manager be aware of what the marketplace offers as well as his or her organization's plans.

The manager should be prepared for the integration of data, voice, and possibly facsimile; he or she should also be well grounded in data communications technology and know what communications functions the company will require and what the coming technology will offer.

2 Perspective on Digital Communications by Richard Parkinson

INTRODUCTION

The North American telephone system, with its rich, innovative history, provides the best telephone service in the world. The system has grown from Alexander Graham Bell's telephone that was patented in March 1876 to the vast network of today, encompassing nearly 150 million telephones in the United States and Canada.

To date, the major use of the telephone network has been the transmission of analog signals—human speech. An analog signal is one that continuously varies; its three characteristics are:

- Amplitude—the power, or loudness, of the signal, measured in decibels, a logarithmic ratio of power
- Frequency—the pitch of the signal, measured in Hertz (cycles per second)
- Phase—a particular point along the sine wave, measured in degrees

Humans detect the amplitude or frequency of a voice as the loudness or the pitch of a sound, respectively. Phase changes cannot be detected by human ears, but they can be detected by electronic equipment.

Transmission Hierarchy

As communicating over long distances became more popular, an alternative to stringing hundreds of copper wires over hundreds of miles was needed. The approach taken was to find a method of using one pair of copper wires to accommodate two or more voice channels at once. Multiplexing several voice channels required understanding the characteristics of speech and the capacity of the open (uninsulated) copper wire in common use.

It was found that a voice signal was strongest within a range of approximately 3,000 Hz; this bandwidth provided sufficient voice tonal quality for the called party to recognize the caller. Attempts in the early 1900s to multiplex these individual voice signals on a copper wire (which had a bandwidth of approximately 150kHz) allowed 12 voice channels (in the middle of the bandwidth), using a nominal voice channel capacity of 4,000 Hz (3,000 Hz for the voice signal and 1,000 Hz as a buffer between adjacent channels). The advent of microwave radio transmission in the late 1940s brought the formulation of a hierarchy of multiplexing, using frequency division to carry several hundred individual voice channels on a very high bandwidth radio frequency (see Figure 2-1).

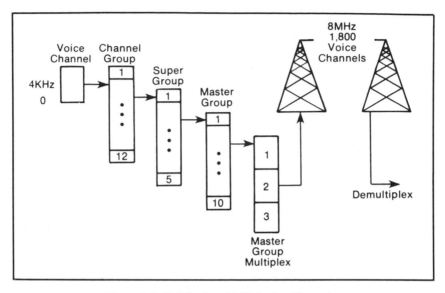

Figure 2-1. Bell System Multiplexing Hierarchy

Switching Hierarchy

As soon as the telecommunications pioneers wanted to intercommunicate, the need for some central connecting arrangement became evident. Initially, this was provided by groups of operators who manually connected callers and called parties (at a building referred to as an exchange). Mechanical alternatives were gradually developed, and the first fully automatic exchange was installed in 1921. It was soon evident that a way of allowing any telephone in the country to orderly and reliably access any other telephone was needed. The wide geographic dispersion and vast numbers of exchanges, however, made it impractical for each exchange to be directly connected to every other exchange.

A hierarchical approach involving five exchange classes was chosen (see Figure 2-2). Class 5 (end office) is the exchange that provides network access to home or office telephones. Calls are routed through these exchanges over various routes, determined in part by the digits dialed and in part by alternate routing schemes, during periods of network congestion. The Class 1 (regional center) is the final option when lower-level offices cannot complete a call over their primary direct routes. A busy signal, indicating that all circuits are busy, implies that even a final-choice route is unavailable. It is interesting that while there are more than 20,000 Class 5 offices serving the 138 million phones in the United States, there are only 10 Class 1 offices.

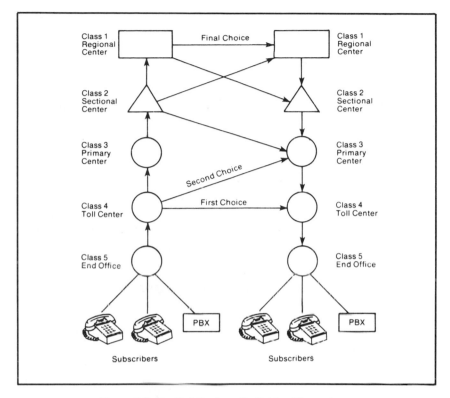

Figure 2-2. North American Switching Hierarchy

Evolution of Switching Technology

The technology used in these exchanges has been marked by three evolutionary milestones. The first automation of telephone switching is credited to Almon Strowger, who patented a switching technique in 1892. The step-by-step method of switching that evolved from this design is still used in many Class 5 offices. A rotary dial generates direct-current pulses to the switches, which sequentially route the call from switch to switch until a final switch (a connector) is reached, providing access to the dialed telephone. The constant wiping action of the wiper arm used to search for a free circuit makes this technique unsuitable for data transmission; it should thus be avoided when possible.

Second Generation. The second generation of switching combined the concept of common control with a crossbar arrangement—an improved mechanical connection that provides faster call set-up time and a cleaner contact mechanism that reduces impulse noise. In this technique, common control connects the call after dialing is complete, using a series of cross-points formed by the joining of horizontal and vertical bars in a crossbar switch frame.

Initially, the control logic used hard-wired logic circuits; it has since evolved to the use of special-purpose computers that control the crossbar mechanism or the newer reed relays, correeds, ferreeds, or solid-state switches that serve as crosspoints.

Third Generation. In the third generation of switching, the concept of computerized common control involves digitizing voice by means of pulse-code modulation, delta modulation, or the like. Time-division multiplexing techniques, in which time slots are matched at high speed, are used to connect two lines. Although this switching method has been used more widely in PBX designs than in telephone central offices, this situation is changing rapidly as an increasing number of digital telephone exchanges are being installed.

The technological evolution of the PBX in all its various forms—basic switchboard service, centrex service, direct inward dial service—has paralleled that of the central offices. The transition from second to third generation was a mid-1970s phenomenon that has seen explosive growth during the past few years, offering new and exciting concepts in communications.

THE TELECOMMUNICATIONS NETWORK TODAY

As previously stated, the telephone network was designed primarily to transmit an analog signal—the human voice. During the past 15 years, the trend has been increasingly to convert the human voice into a digital bit stream so that it can be switched and transmitted digitally. Pulse-code modulation is the most popular method of converting a voice signal to a digital signal. Figure 2-3 shows the three basic steps involved in analog-to-digital conversion. The desire

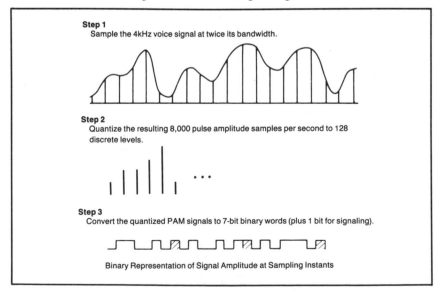

Step 1
Sample the 4kHz voice signal at twice its bandwidth.

Step 2
Quantize the resulting 8,000 pulse amplitude samples per second to 128 discrete levels.

Step 3
Convert the quantized PAM signals to 7-bit binary words (plus 1 bit for signaling).

Binary Representation of Signal Amplitude at Sampling Instants

Figure 2-3. Pulse-Code Modulation

to multiplex multiple voice channels over copper wire (and ultimately micro-wave radio and satellite) using digital transmission (see Table 2-1) led to the development of a new multiplexing hierarchy (see Figure 2-4).

Table 2-1. Digital Carriers

Carrier Description	Bit Rate (bps)	No. of Voice Channels
	64K	1
T1	1.544M	24
T2	6.312M	96
T3	44.736M	672
T3a	89.472M	1,344
T4	274.176M	4,032

Current Use of Digital Technology

The trend to digital transmission and switching has been accelerating at an ever-increasing rate. At a recent network symposium, an AT&T network-planning vice-president cited some statistics concerning the Bell System's current status in using digital transmission and switching:

- Approximately 100 million circuit miles of twisted-pair, coaxial, or fiber-optic T-carrier cable are now in use.
- Approximately 5 million circuit miles of digital radio links use micro-wave and satellite technology.
- Approximately 250,000 subscriber-carrier local loops now use digital transmission.
- Approximately 100 toll-switching offices and 900 Class 5 end offices now use digital time-division switching systems.

This use of digital technology by the Bell System is paralleled, in varying degrees, by carriers outside the United States. Users should be aware that the vast analog systems and the capital investment in these holdings preclude any rapid change to all-digital technology. Although such changes are currently underway and will increase, the initial changes will remain limited in scope.

Network Signaling

One particularly interesting development that has resulted from computer-ized common control and digital switching is an enhanced method of network signaling. This relatively new approach, common-channel interoffice signaling (CCIS), promises many features and services not previously available. Signal-ing is required to allow calls to be connected through the many switching offices that may be involved in a call of any distance. Before the introduction of CCIS, every trunk line between two exchanges required equipment at each end to generate or accept dialing information. This sequential passing of dialing information through every exchange involved causes a call set-up delay of up to 20 seconds between the last digit dialed and the first ring. In contrast, CCIS uses a separate data channel network and a form of packet switching so that call set-up takes only a fraction of that time, typically from one to three seconds.

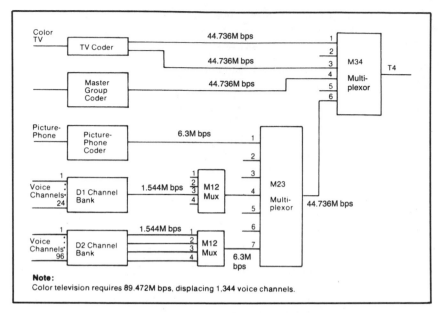

Figure 2-4. U.S. and Canadian Digital Hierarchy

Currently, the Bell System is using CCIS signaling for 25 to 30 percent of the connections in its toll network; Bell is committed to extending such use further into the switching hierarchy (including PBXs) as rapidly as possible. A CCITT recommendation (No. 7 [1]) should stimulate compatible worldwide support for CCIS.

PBXs Today

Supplying digital PBX equipment has become a fiercely competitive business, and several dozen domestic and foreign manufacturers are producing an ever-increasing number of features—faster than the user community can absorb them. Whether the PBX is a standalone system or part of a corporate network, it is increasingly considered for use in switching data as well as voice communications. Most digital PBXs are designed for the characteristics of voice telephone use: three to five minutes holding time, approximately half internal and half external calling, and an average busy-hour use per instrument of 10 minutes. These characteristics have allowed PBX designers to have concentration levels within the switching network at typically a 3:1 ratio. Calling patterns that differ from the normal voice application, as they do with data transmission, frequently cause service degradation.

The most recent PBX designs use a nonblocking concept in which every line, whether local or trunk, can be in use simultaneously. Almost all nonblocking PBXs use digital switching so that a 10,000-line PBX would be capable of switching five hundred 64K-bit-per-second conversions. A few PBX manufacturers currently offer simultaneous voice and data switching for in-house applications, as an alternative to using port contention devices. It is essential to understand the full cost and operational implications of using a PBX designed with network contention for data switching. The cost equation should include such items as:

- Wiring and cable.
- Hardware in the PBX common equipment cabinets.
- Hardware at the user terminal location. A more costly telephone set, for example, might be necessary to connect the data terminal equipment (DTE).
- The software upgrade required to support data transmission.
- Reduction of the quantity of lines and trunks to minimize congestion in the switching matrix.

Current Corporate Networks

When two or more PBX systems are connected to allow voice calling between them, organizations often rent dedicated lines to connect the PBXs, thereby providing an alternative to regular long-distance service. These tie lines (or trunks) allow a local on one PBX to call a local on the other by dialing fewer digits than would be involved in direct distance dialing—and without operator involvement.

The following call set-up example, illustrated in Figure 2-5, indicates how calls are currently routed over more private networks. PBX local 2222 in San Francisco would use the following dialing procedure to call local 5555 in Minneapolis: dial 7, wait for dial tone from the Denver PBX; dial 7, wait for dial tone from Chicago; dial 7, wait for dial tone from Minneapolis; then dial local 5555. Obviously, if any link between San Francisco and Minneapolis were busy, the call would be blocked and the caller would have to hang up and try again or use some alternate route. These tie lines are still predominantly analog, necessitating the use of modems when lines are used for data transmission.

Some of the Bell Systems' very large customers use specially designed network services such as the enhanced private switching communications service (EPSCS). Special Bell switching equipment is used for EPSCS, and such enhanced features as uniform numbering and automatic alternate routing are provided. The line interface, however, is still generally analog between the customer's on-site equipment and the Bell exchange.

Other Communications Technologies

Although twisted-pair copper wire, coaxial cable, and terrestrial microwave are the most commonly used methods of transmission for both analog and digital signals, the use of satellites and fiber-optic cable is increasing. Satellite and fiber-optic transmission offer certain advantages over traditional methods. Satellite transmission, for example, provides high bandwidth and broadcast capability, and earth stations can be located virtually anywhere. Fiber-optic cables also offer high bandwidth; they are immune to electromagnetic interference, and they provide a high degree of safety from tapping.

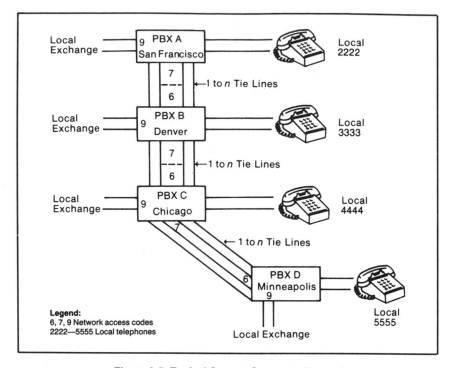

Figure 2-5. Typical Current Corporate Network

THE FUTURE TELECOMMUNICATIONS NETWORK

As the demand for increased bandwidth grows, so does the trend toward all-digital transmission, with the telephone network well on its way to becoming totally digital. The concepts and services of this evolving digital network should be considered in current planning for networks that are to be implemented during the next two to three years. Networks of the future will encompass switching, local area networking, and the integration of voice and data.

Packet Switching

Packet-switching networks have, of course, been in use for several years. The CCITT X.25 Recommendation serves as a common base for the design of generally compatible software and hardware. The two U.S. public packet-switched networks, Telenet and TYMNET, provide such service as a cost-effective alternative to dedicated or switched service from the Bell System or equivalent common carriers. GTE-Telenet, Tymnet, and several other suppliers of communications processors also market private packet-switching network hardware and software that allow companies to use private packet networks for data transmission.

Although the use of packet switching for voice has been the subject of considerable experimentation and research during the past several years, many industry people feel an acceptable-quality packet voice switch is at least seven to ten years away. For example, approximately 250 packets per second per conversation would need to be processed, and large amounts of memory are required to store packets in transit. The variable delay in a network would affect the intonation and meaning of some phrases, and during periods of network congestion, delays of several hundred milliseconds would occur, causing considerable negative user reaction.

Packet-switched voice is an appealing concept that is worth watching; it offers the theoretical potential to double the use of long-distance facilities. Studies have shown that a typical voice conversation involves 40 percent talking, 10 percent thinking, and 50 percent listening. The traditional circuit-switched network (whether analog or digital) requires a physical full-duplex path through the network. Thus, while one person is talking, the return path from the listener is idle. Packetized voice would permit use of this return path, effectively doubling the path's utilization.

Local Area Networks

Local area networks (LANs) are currently the subject of considerable research and many technical papers. Conceptually, a local area network is a common highway over which data between two devices is routed. Such networks are currently being used in such small geographic areas as manufacturing complexes and universities, connecting a few—or thousands of—terminals. Although most local area networks are still considered experimental, several companies, such as 3M and Amdax, are now offering turnkey systems. The LAN interface unit provides both network protocol and terminal device support. This concept will require three to four years before it matures to the level of packet switching.

Integration of Voice and Data

It has become essential for users to maximize efficiency and minimize costs with their telecommunications networks. Traditionally, the voice network lines and switching equipment have been minimally used for data transmission. Voice lines are used during off-hours, or the lines are used alternately for voice and data. Most data transmission today uses dedicated analog or digital lines, packet networks, or other specialized common-carrier services designed specifically for data transmission. Electronic mail, store-and-forward message switching, facsimile, and other such services generally use equipment designed for that purpose.

An alternative to having separate voice and data networks is to integrate them, and, for now at least, the digital PBX appears to be the preferred network integrator. (An office supercontroller can potentially integrate all office communications functions.) Once voice, the predominant user of communications lines, is digitized, it effectively becomes digital data. Current voice digitization uses a 64K-bit-per-second transmission rate, which is considered high speed for data terminals.

Figure 2-6 shows some of the components that will be part of corporate networks of the future, including the following key items:

• Sophisticated interface units to connect and support:
   —Analog rotary and Touch-Tone™ telephones
   —Digital telephones, with or without data terminal support capability (a digital telephone includes an analog-to-digital conversion codec)
   —A data terminal interface unit to serve many protocols, codes, and asynchronous and synchronous devices (including a packet assembler-disassembler function, if required)
   —A T1-compatible interface to multiplex 24 or more voice channels directly onto a T1 link

• Sophisticated software products to provide:
   —Statistical multiplexing or packet switching over the inter-PBX digital links
   —Support of CCITT Recommendations X.25, X.28, X.29, and/or X.3, plus the software necessary to perform the functions of a packet-switched node (e.g., flow control, congestion control, alternate routing)
   —Support of the CCIS signaling system for voice and possibly data switching

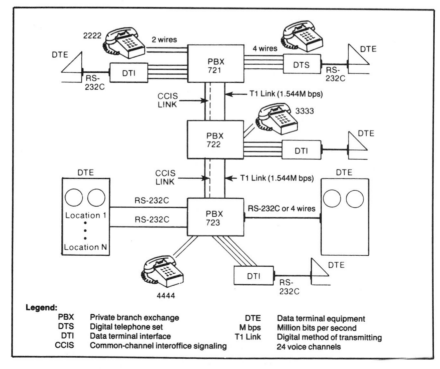

Figure 2-6. Future Corporate Network Components

The major cost will be for hardware and the associated software to support the multitude of terminals using the integrated network, ranging from ASCII-asynchronous to SNA-synchronous devices, each requiring unique handling.

In terms of cost, it must be realized that the value of the PBX or controller supporting the network is in the elimination of separate switching hardware and the potential for reduced wiring to each terminal location. Using the PBX for data switching will provide the enhanced reliability traditionally available with telephone switching systems. With the use of redundant processors, memories, and the like, a figure of 15 to 20 years between catastrophic failures is commonly quoted.

Today's network designers must understand switching concepts, transmission techniques, engineering, data transmission concepts, link protocols, computer-network architectures and design concepts, and traffic engineering—in addition to being able to accommodate user needs. Unfortunately, such a superperson does not exist, and a team effort is required to incorporate these essential disciplines into any major network plan.

The lack of T1 digital links is the major impediment to effective integration of voice and data, and users must put pressure on the common carriers to provide such links between all their corporate network locations. A few of the reasons for this lack of T1 interface connections are valid, most are unwarranted, and all are resolvable.

The Value of Digital Communications

Users frequently ask what will benefit them in the trend toward digital communications. The answers to this question depend on the availability of hardware and/or facilities from the telecommunications vendors. (In some cases, the provider benefits directly, with the user reaping secondary benefits.) The advantages of digital communications include the following:
- LSI and VLSI circuitry is inexpensive and compact, allowing reductions in size of several orders of magnitude.
- Digital circuitry is less complex and more reliable than the equivalent analog circuitry.
- Digital transmission is less sensitive to signal fading caused by such things as differing moisture and temperature layers, attenuation from fog or rain, and reflections from buildings. It can also use portions of the radio spectrum that analog transmission cannot.
- Digital signals are regenerated rather than amplified (as with analog signals). This eliminates noise accumulation and provides users with a higher-quality voice signal.
- In tandem networks, analog PBXs introduce a three-decibel loss at each tandem point, thus limiting their number in a network connection. A digital PBX incurs no loss and thus allows many more tandem points, with improved voice quality.

CONCLUSION

The move from analog to digital communications continues to expand and accelerate. Digital technology offers the advantages of smaller packaging, higher reliability, superior transmission quality, better utilization of resources, and, what may be most important, far greater adaptability to new demands for services. CCIS signaling, for example, vastly improves call set-up time, and, as digital T1 links become more readily available, data transmission users will be able to obtain a 64K-bit-per-second transmission path for the same price now paid for a 4KHz, 9,600-bit-per-second path, providing greater speed at lower cost.

As costs for higher bandwidth decrease, it may be possible to set up teleconferencing connections as easily as today's three-party voice conference. Another valuable service made possible by digital technology is voice mail, using every telephone as an I/O device. As with electronic mail, users can input to and receive messages from a "mailbox." Voice messages are digitally encoded and stored for delivery as appropriate. Although memory requirements are high (a 10-second message requires the storage equivalent of 80,000 characters), decreasing memory costs are making this service economically feasible.

The opportunities that will eventually be made possible by all-digital telecommunications technology are just now beginning to appear. What the future will bring may be limited only by the imagination.

Note:
1. Information regarding this and other CCITT recommendations can be obtained from American National Standards Institute, 1430 Broadway, New York NY 10018.

③ Formulating Network Requirements

by Pete Moulton

INTRODUCTION

Although many people within an organization may be willing to discuss network requirements generally, very few are willing to assume responsibility or make decisions in this area. Managers who are unfamiliar with data communications and computer systems may feel they are committing themselves irretrievably when they define any quantified requirements. Thus, they may be reluctant to identify or formulate data communications requirements. Once the requirements are identified and described in a planning document, however, the same managers feel free to criticize: now they can think of exceptions to the rule that make the projections invalid and that will certainly produce an understated or overstated load.

Because information on communications load requirements becomes available only after the network is operational, estimates of these requirements must be used. These projections can be made with increasing accuracy during each step of the process if they are cataloged by application and constantly reviewed and revised by operating and system design personnel.

Data Communications System Life Cycle

The life cycle of a data communications system is an important planning consideration; technological changes will have to be dealt with during the system's useful life. Each network is a representation of the technology at the time of its design and implementation; it becomes obsolete when new products and services based upon new technologies that cannot be incorporated into the existing network provide greatly enhanced system reliability, reduced costs, and additional applications.

During the course of its life cycle, a data communications system passes through the phases shown in Figure 3-1:

- Requirements definition—The computer applications and information systems that will use the system are identified and described.
- Design—The hardware, software, and services from which the system will be constructed are specified. The structure and layout of the network are determined during the design phase.

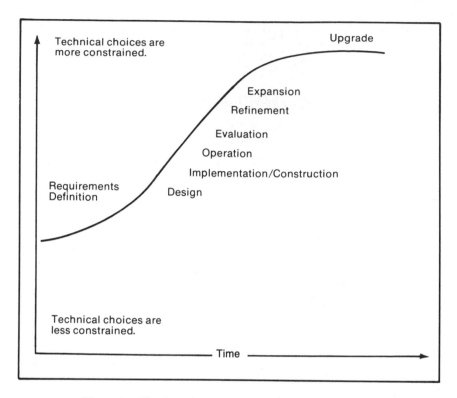

Figure 3-1. The Data Communications System Life Cycle

- Construction/implementation—The communications hardware, software, and services are ordered, and the system is built. When enough work has been completed, a phase-in of the new system and a phase-out of the old system are begun.
- Operation—This begins in earnest after the data communications system is phased in. At this point, all the minute design oversights should be identified and corrected.
- Evaluation—Once operation is stabilized, the system's performance in terms of reliability, response time (transmission delay), capacity, and cost is evaluated.
- Refinement—The results of the evaluation phase are used to refine the network's structure.
- Expansion—As the computer applications and information systems gain wider use within the organization, the data communications system is expanded to accommodate new sites and increased information volumes.
- Upgrade—This last phase begins a repetition of the entire life-cycle process for the next-generation system.

The life-cycle concept can be applied to a data communications system as a whole or in part. A large system, for example, can be divided into nationwide

and local service areas. One part of the system can support nationwide communications and another only communications within a small geographic area, a
building, or a facility. In addition, each portion of the data communications
system can be in a different life-cycle phase.

As a data communications network moves through these phases, the network planner becomes more constrained in the design alternatives that can be
used to provide increased capacity, support new applications, and resolve
operational problems. Such restrictions are caused by the difficulty and cost of
changing an operational data communications network. Significant short-term
changes cannot be justified because they usually provide a low return on
investment. A longer return-on-investment time for an upgrade allows consideration of a broader range of design alternatives.

Role of Requirements Definition in Network Planning

Requirements definition is the first step in the network planning process (see
Figure 3-2) and forms the basis for all subsequent network design. If require-

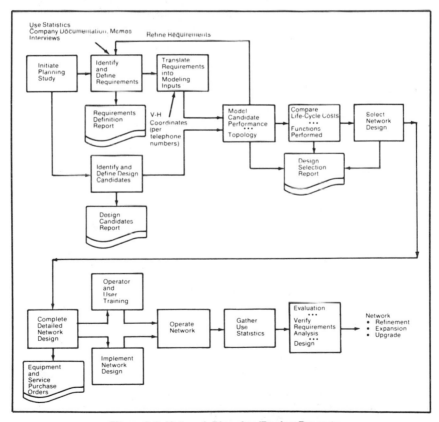

Figure 3-2. Network Planning/Design Process

ments are misstated, disorganized, or based on inadequate information, the resultant network will be poorly designed. The definition process and common-sense checking of the results thus become a key element in the network planning process.

Requirements definition is a distinct task that has specific input and a defined output; the output, a requirements definition report, serves as a focus for all participants in this process. It frequently prompts further data input and refinements. During preparation of the report, a logical review and commonsense analysis of the input data are performed and documented to ensure that the requirements data adequately represents network requirements without over-stating them.

The flow of activities in the requirements definition process is shown in Figure 3-3. The raw data is sought from all available sources; it can be categorized by site, type of equipment or service, vendor, or other classification. The gathered data is organized and formulated using the requirements data preparation (RDP) forms (Appendix A). The data is then extracted from the RDP forms for analysis and comparison to check its validity. Errors and overstatements are corrected and entered on the forms. The data is then summarized, and inputs for network modeling are prepared.

GATHERING INPUT DATA

Gathering input data begins with interviewing the personnel involved in the data communications network. These interviews are used to develop a precise definition of present DP and telecommunications systems, to uncover current problems, and to tailor the data-gathering process to the available data. This process emphasizes the information that is directly relevant to the network planning and design process. Data collection should focus on obtaining engineering and operational specifics since the results of computer modeling and evaluation are only as good as the data used. Data collection covers three areas:

- Terminal locations
- The types of communications facilities and the host computer systems
- The future DP and communications requirements of the network users

The categories of data supplied for network analysis should be precisely defined, containing, at a minimum, a list of the terminal and host processor sites, including the following for each terminal and host processor:

- Terminals
    —Location (city/state)
    —Average monthly traffic volume (to and from)
    —Terminal speed
    —Number of terminals
    —Data destination(s)
    —Terminal installation date (actual or expected)
- Host Processors
    —Location (city/state)

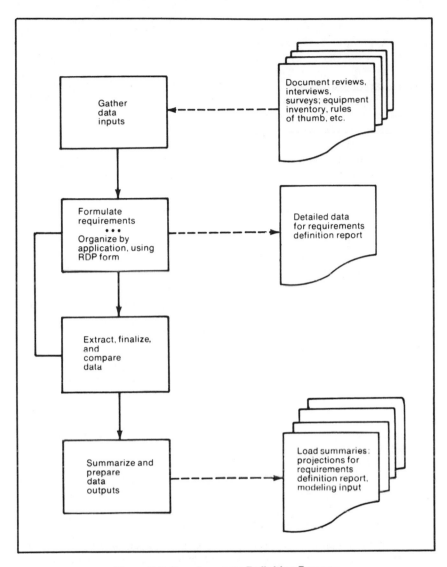

Figure 3-3. Requirements Definition Process

With only minimal data, a number of significant assumptions, such as the distribution of the traffic load over the hours of each day in the month, must be made to complete the planning analysis and modeling. The use of such assumptions can be significantly reduced if additional data is available; for example:

- Terminal Sites
  - Telephone area code
  - Serving central office
  - Hours of operation
  - Peak activity hours

    —Average number of daily calls (originated and received)
    —Average call length (connect time)
    —Average characters transmitted
    —Average characters received
- Host processor sites
    —Telephone area code
    —Serving central office
    —Hours of operation
    —Peak activity hours
    —Volume of data processed (average and peak, in transactions per hour and characters per hour)

Input data for the requirements definition process can come from several sources. The five common data-gathering sources are:
- Document reviews
- Interviews
- Surveys and questionnaires
- Literature searches
- Experience estimates (rules of thumb)

Reviewing technical reports and documents (particularly invoices from vendors and common carriers and systems performance reports) can provide detailed insight into the operation of an existing network. Among the information to be gleaned from such reviews are the exact locations of terminals, multiplexors, and so forth; technical characteristics of the data communications equipment, including transmission rates, options, codes; and current network equipment or service costs. This information is sometimes incomplete, and direct interviews with operating personnel and on-site visits (especially to sites with heavy user concentration and installed equipment) are necessary for verification. When extensive on-site surveys and interviews are beyond both the requirement for precision and the budget, surveys or questionnaires can be used to develop the information. The accuracy and detail of the information obtained through surveys are less reliable than those of data gathered through direct interviews: surveys and questionnaires are frequently not completed. Direct telephone contact with remote-site personnel can be used to verify survey entries and to complete the data entries.

Equipment capabilities are frequently developed through a literature search. Corporate library facilities and commercial technology reports provide detailed functional descriptions and cost data on various data communications equipment. It is sometimes necessary, however, to augment such information through direct vendor contact.

Estimates based on experience or rules of thumb can also be used to develop input data for network analysis. If it were necessary, for example, to determine the amount of data input at the network communications control computers, one could use experience with line protocols, RJE operations, CRT terminals, and teletypewriter operation to develop direct-line efficiency factors. These factors are then multiplied by the maximum data rate for the channels and summed over all channels to help make more accurate estimates.

Combining the use of questionnaires and survey techniques with follow-up interviews to gather and validate the data on the existing computer and communications systems may enable involving some field DP personnel in the network planning project. This demonstrates to the field people a continued management interest in DP problems. The field personnel must, however, be encouraged to participate fully in developing accurate and complete data and in providing insight and ideas that cannot be obtained from questionnaires.

When the time is available, interview techniques and forms should be tested at a trial site so that they can be tailored to the specific data-gathering requirements. Extremely detailed data is not generally necessary to perform the analysis, and time is often not sufficient for testing the questionnaires and interview techniques. Thus, suitably tailored, simple, straightforward data-gathering methods are frequently used, and more detailed data is gathered later as required. When the data-gathering package is complete, data gathering and validation for all network sites can proceed quickly.

Input data should be developed as early as possible; if it is incomplete, a decision must be made whether to proceed with the data available or wait for additional information. The planner, for example, may want to compare costs between present data communications services and the proposed network. If actual cost figures are unavailable, representative costs can sometimes be estimated by modeling. In this case, site utilization data should be developed for modeling and evaluation. Such output alone is frequently useful to network planners.

FORMULATING REQUIREMENTS

Data communications needs stem from a mixture of existing computer programs, almost-operational systems, and planned activities: these can all be associated with applications. Data communications operational descriptions are formulated for each application, using a standardized RDP form. These descriptions are based on the data and documentation developed during data gathering.

Computer Applications

The basic concept underlying the formulation of data communications requirements is that of a computer application, that is, computer software and a data base operating on computer hardware (most often in conjunction with a vendor-developed operating system), terminals, and communications facilities to assist in the performance of diverse work functions.

Formulating data communications requirements relates computer applications and information systems to terminal and communications hardware, communications software, and the common-carrier services that will transfer the input and output data from and to the locations where they are generated, processed, and used. As a result, a major objective in formulating requirements is to identify the work activities that are or will be automated and to relate those activities to the information input and output, the medium (e.g., paper, cards) on which the information resides, and the geographic locations where the information is generated/processed/used. Once identified, each application must be assigned the specific hardware on which it will be implemented. A retailing application, for example, may use an optical wand to collect product inventory information from already-tagged merchandise in the company's stores.

Because data communications networks serve many applications, the volume of information for all applications must be combined to determine the network design. Transforming the raw data into requirements for specific applications helps identify applications and associated data volumes that were not uncovered in the data-gathering process; this activity also helps develop the network's total information volume.

Requirements Data Preparation Form

The RDP form covers the following areas:
- Disclaimer—The interviews conducted with personnel concerned with the application are reviewed and summarized to develop a description of the computer application. Frequently, these people do not feel safe with the projections and statements and become concerned because they may have to live with the results of their estimates. The disclaimer statement is therefore used to reduce such anxiety.
- Application identification—This defines the formal name (and its associated acronym) of the computer application described in the RDP form.
- Application description—This is a statement of what the application does and what it is intended to accomplish.
- Benefits of the application—These are the positive contributions of the application in the overall functioning of the organization.
- Current status—This area of the form describes the application's current state of development. A system may be operational, under development, or planned.
- References—This area of the form lists memos, reports, and other source documents and materials that describe the system or application. These source documents and materials should be compiled in a bibliography.
- Data communications operational description—This identifies the type of data communications application (e.g., remote batch, inquiry/ response, time sharing, administrative message-switching), the primary user group, input and output message sizes, the overall traffic load for the application, the peak traffic load, the type of terminal hardware, and the special output medium. A brief description of the current application operation is then developed.
- Data privacy and security requirements—Privacy deals with the distribution limitations of the data in the system; security describes the mechanisms or preventive measures that must be taken to ensure that the data base is not violated.
- Application availability—Availability is the amount of time that the application must be in operation and accessible to the users.

- Response time—This indicates how quickly requests input to the application must be answered (e.g., within three seconds, monthly). In some cases, turnaround time may be more descriptive.
- Reliability—This deals with the percentage of available time during which the system must not fail. Reliability should also include a description of such consequences of a failure as the cost of a work load backlog.
- Data communications load—Assumptions are usually made in deriving the data communications load for the application. Typical assumptions are the annual percentage growth rate, the number of transactions occurring on an annual basis, the ratio of the peak-hour load to the average hourly load, the number of peak hours in a given day, and the input and output message sizes for each transaction. Load calculations are used to project the total communications traffic during the system's life cycle. The final step is to determine the ratio of peak-hour traffic to the total daily traffic. Appendix A shows a technique based on the assumptions that peak-hour traffic is 10 times that of average hourly traffic and that there are three hours of peak traffic each day.
- Geographic distribution of terminals—This is merely a listing of the locations serviced by the application and the number of terminals at each location. To complete the network topological analysis, the peak hourly load must be distributed over all sites serviced by the application. In cases where there is no actual usage data available, this distribution is usually performed by assuming that each terminal has an equivalent load.

The application requirements identified on the individual RDP forms are summarized by assigning the average load to each terminal location for each application. The average and peak loads for all applications at each location are summarized, producing an overall load that must be handled by the data communications system. Verification of the data communications system requirements now begins.

An abbreviated Requirements Data Preparation form is shown in Appendix B. The exact structure and some of the information content of the form are, of course, dependent upon the planning objectives and the input data available. The forms presented in this chapter are examples of forms that have been used successfully in data communications planning studies.

USING THE OUTPUT

Validation and evaluation of the data formulated with the RDP forms should address such questions as the time dependence of terminals (e.g., do terminals transmit critical data at 8:00 A.M. or at 9:00 A.M.?) as well as idiosyncracies in the data (e.g., two terminals in the same building with very little use in the same month).

This requirements formulation necessitates using a top-down approach, presenting each step of the analysis within the context of a complete overview. Because applications and their operations are often in the process of definition, the network requirements overview should be based on the parameters and operational characteristics presented in the RDP forms.

Data communications loads can thus be projected prior to the completion of feasibility studies for specific applications. It should be noted that the studies can modify the operational characteristics of the planned systems and that load projections and planned systems may change. Therefore, the descriptions developed in the RDP forms should be viewed as conceptual rather than actual system designs. Changes in the descriptions are frequently not significant enough to invalidate the planning guidelines developed. The simplification and documentation of the analysis made possible by the RDP forms allow further validation or replication of each step in the network planning process as improved data becomes available. When analysis of the information reveals inconsistencies in the planning data provided, such inconsistencies should be removed with guidance from user personnel.

Analyses and Summaries

Applications data is summarized to produce aggregate data communications requirements; the overall data communications requirement is concisely described by an annual traffic load in millions (or billions) of characters. This aggregated data communications traffic load can be distributed into geographic areas. These areas may have significance as regional operating boundaries for administrative, managerial, and work load allocation purposes, or they can be based on other criteria.

Another crucial parameter in data communications traffic analysis is peak-hour traffic (i.e., the average load transmitted during the hour of greatest activity each day). Time-zone segregation of a geographically widespread network would permit hourly analysis of the host-computer or central-site load over an entire day, indicating the several peak times.

Data communications requirements can be analyzed graphically to determine the dominant applications; the graphs would show changes as other applications become more significant.

The equipment used to service high-speed synchronous communications terminals differs from the equipment used to serve lower-speed asynchronous communications terminals. Network analysis and design, therefore, separates the load for each type of terminal. Because applications commonly use a single terminal type, analysis of the data by application helps to identify the high- and low-speed, synchronous and asynchronous loads that the network will service. Separate subnetworks to support these loads are combined manually during the final design analysis into the overall data communications network that will support all applications.

Validity of the data is checked by developing comparisons between the load and the planned terminal installations over the geographic areas that the network is to service. Consistency and increased validity in the data are attained when a degree of correlation exists between the geographic terminal and data distribution (particularly if each was developed independently). Table 3-1 illustrates such a comparison.

Table 3-1. Load/Terminal Distribution Comparison

	No. of Terminals	%	Annual Load	%	Peak-Hour Load	%
FY80						
Area 1	30	20.13	693.6	21.15	284.7	19.25
2	22	14.77	485.6	14.81	228.8	15.47
3	27	18.12	665.7	20.30	279.8	18.92
4	7	4.70	136.2	4.15	61.4	4.15
5	25	16.78	583.8	17.80	240.6	16.27
6	38	25.50	714.4	21.79	383.8	25.94
FY85						
Area 1	40	20.93	1,328.7	20.31	710.5	18.88
2	32	16.79	1,142.5	17.47	688.2	18.29
3	35	18.32	1,370.8	20.96	729.9	19.40
4	9	4.71	273.5	4.18	177.3	4.71
5	35	18.32	1,189.2	18.18	616.7	16.39
6	40	20.93	1,238.9	18.90	840.0	22.33
FY90						
Area 1	178	22.50	2,855.3	21.91	1,758.5	20.98
2	88	11.15	1,688.5	12.96	937.2	11.18
3	212	26.87	3,381.0	25.94	2,266.1	27.04
4	90	11.41	1,094.7	8.40	842.9	10.06
5	98	12.42	1,974.1	15.15	1,117.9	13.34
6	123	15.59	2,040.8	15.64	1,458.6	17.40

Data Use

Effective use of the information gathered is essential to the analysis and planning steps that follow the identification and formulation effort. Some of the important requirements are the operational description of the data communications applications, definition of the data bases, and timing of the applications.

Data Communications Operational Descriptions. These descriptions provide insight into the hardware and software system components used, in terms of their specific types, performance, and cost. For example, a network using multiplexors that serve several remote sites may be configured, with a single cross-country line to a host computer facility. The data communications operational description would identify the types of hardware and software components in this system design. In later, more detailed planning phases, different multiplexors could be evaluated for their operational characteristics (e.g., the ability to determine network malfunctions, gather traffic statistics, and diagnose remote multiplexors from the central site) and communications load capacity. The operational descriptions also play a key role in determining the overall network design alternatives, which are used in the topological analysis to determine the best and least-cost network design.

Definition of the Application Data Bases. This is another important requirement that includes specifying the data inputs by describing their sources, formats, information content, and media. The data verification, processing, and storage and retrieval functions performed upon the data bases are also identified and described, and the data outputs are specified. This specification should include the destination, format, and contents of the output as well as the medium upon which it is to be displayed. Explicit specification can help develop an overall consistency between the data bases that will permit their integration into more comprehensive applications. The objective is to do so without completely redesigning the organization's data base.

Timing. Timing is also a critical requirement. Because many organizations have limited resources for implementing and developing computer applications, the development and implementation of each application area is similarly limited. Applications should therefore be ranked in terms of their contribution and implementation priority. This ranking, together with manpower estimates, can then be used to determine the timing for development and implementation.

Network Modeling

One of the major uses for requirements data is in developing the network topology. The load and site data described on the RDP forms is used to prepare inputs to network modeling tools (software programs that model the network mathematically). The operational descriptions can be combined with current communications service offerings (e.g., TYMNET, Telenet) to develop topological design alternatives. Trade-offs are usually made between these specialized communications services and the more traditional measured-use and full-period services (e.g., WATS and the AT&T multischedule private-line offerings) combined with packaged communications hardware and software offerings from computer equipment vendors.

Each data communications system design alternative is mathematically modeled for performance and then for cost, using current tariffs and the geographically distributed peak loads described in the RDP forms. This modeling provides an overall performance capacity and cost analysis for each network design alternative. Recommendation of a network design to be implemented is based upon the least-cost alternative modeled, provided that all alternatives modeled have been reasonably assessed for ease of sign-on, maintainability, technical feasibility, reliability, and so forth, (cost outputs from these modeling programs can also be used to develop annual budgeting estimates).

Once the overall network topology has been determined (using the network analysis tools), it is manually refined to ensure the desired levels of reliability and maintainability. The mathematical modeling, for example, might place a hubbing center in a city where within-the-hour maintenance services are not available. In this case, it would be better to incur the additional costs of reconfiguring the communications system in order to place the hubbing center in a larger city, where one-hour service is available. In another instance, the output of the network models may be modified to increase reliability. When a hub site interfaces a large number of remote sites, it may be better for the supporting trunk to be implemented in an AT&T Digital Dataphone Service

(DDS) trunk rather than in an analog trunk line. Although this would increase the cost of the trunk, it would provide increased reliability.

Because most network modeling tools are limited in their capabilities to analyze the various data communications requirements, they typically model one aspect of the system analysis, such as low-speed data communications between terminals and the host. Modeling of the high-speed load is performed in subsequent iterations. The results of these analyses are then combined, a process that frequently uncovers additional cost reductions. The output of the network analysis is thus further refined to produce a final network topology.

CONCLUSION

This chapter has presented an approach to formulating data communications network requirements and organizing the requirements, by application, on appropriate forms. These forms structure the data communications requirements and relate them to terminal equipment, organizational benefits, development status, performance parameters, and other factors. This structure sets up comparative analyses and validations of the input data, helps establish priorities in application development, and enables the use of network modeling in the final stages of network planning and design.

APPENDIX A

Requirements Data Preparation Form (RDP)

The data documenting the MIS application described in these forms represents the descriptive information available on this application as of _____, 19 _____. This data has been augmented by assumptions to provide sufficient input for subsequent comparative analyses of data communications strategies.

Application Identification

Master File (MF) System

Description

The Master File (MF) System is a central index to the decentralized casework files, which are maintained in remote offices. The law requires that a central index containing relevant identifying and status information on all casework be maintained. Compliance with the law is achieved through the Master File (MF) System.

Benefits

The system increases caseworker productivity by providing timely status information or all casework. Better and more effective service is effected through increased information consistency, accuracy, and timeliness. An upgraded system would further reduce the manpower expended in tracking and locating casework files; it would also increase control and reduce the incidence of lost files.

Current Status

Operational ___X___   Under Development _____   Date _____

An automated system having online video displays at the host-computer facility is currently operational. This system is undergoing expansion to contain more data and to permit access from remote sites.

Conversion of manual files, containing detailed data, to automated files is being completed. A feasibility test interconnecting additional teletypewriter terminals used for message switching to the MF system is being performed. Installation of enhanced-function video display and teleprinter terminals is planned for 1985. A fully upgraded system with expanded online records is planned for implementation by 1990.

References

Bibliography Sources: (1), (5), (8), (12), and (19).
Applicable Standards: FIPS Publications

Data Communications Operational Description

Type: Offline Data Entry _____ Interactive _X__
               Remote Batch _____ Other _____
User: Administration and Casework Agencywide
Message Size: Input: 250 Characters   Output: 350 Characters
Traffic Load: Average: 3.4 million transactions   Peak: 10 times load

Hardware: Terminal Type: <u>Online</u>   Hardcopy: <u>No</u>
                      <u>Video CRT</u>   Disk: <u>No</u>
                      _____   Magnetic Tape: <u>No</u>
                      _____   Other: <u>No</u>

The Master File System is an information retrieval system with online video and teleprinter terminals located at regional, district, and SMSA casework offices. Central-site operators now enter transactions on the casework files to update, query, post, and purge a central master file. The upgraded system could allow regional and district site operators to perform the update, query, and post transactions. Specified screen format of data will be processed when retrieving file entries. About 250 input characters and 350 output characters would be transmitted during each transaction between the requesting terminal and the host computer system.

Data Privacy and Security

The system must be secure enough to inhibit unauthorized changes or additions to the data files. Dissemination of the data would be restricted to organizational personnel with a need to know.

Availability, Response Time, and Reliability

The system must operate 24 hours a day, seven days a week. Response to queries must average four seconds or less with 99 percent of the responses being six seconds or less. The system must be 98 percent reliable. The cost of outages would be increased work backlog.

Data Communications Load Derivation

1. **Assumptions:**
    Estimated Annual Percentage Growth <u>3</u>
    The 1976 total transactions for the Master File System was 3.37 million. This was derived from data received from the MIS group.

    The peak-hour load is 10 times the average load; there are three hours of peak traffic daily.

    Each transaction has 250 characters of input data and 350 characters of output data.

2. **Load Calculations**
    The Master File System communications load is estimated as follows:
    a. Input and output characters are combined in a transaction to yield 600 characters of data exchanged in each transaction.
    b. The load in 1978 equals
    $$(3.37 \text{ million transactions}) \times (600 \text{ characters})$$
    $$=$$
    $$2.022 \text{ billion characters}$$
    c. The 1978 load is projected to 1980, 1985, and 1990 by using the growth percentage compounded:
    $$2{,}022 \times (1.03)^n = \text{Projected Load}$$

3. **Load Projections**
   Communications load measured in billions of characters

Year	1980	1985	1990
Annual Load	2.14	2.49	2.88

4. **Peak-Hour Transmission Load**
   Restating the assumptions—The system operates 24 hours a day, seven days a week, with a peak-hour load 10 times the average load and three peak-traffic hours each day.

   These assumptions lead to determining the following peak-hour ratio:

Hour	1	2	3	4	5	....	24	
Load weight	10	10	10	1	1	....	1	Sum of weights 51

   Thus, the ratio of peak-hour traffic to total daily traffic is 10:51.

Terminal Distribution

Projected Master File System terminal locations are:

Location	Number of Terminals
Washington DC	35
Baltimore MD	2
•	•
•	•
•	•
•	•
•	•
•	•
Los Angeles CA	16
Phoenix AZ	2
Total for 1980	327
Detroit MI	2
Miami FL	2
•	•
•	•
•	•
New Orleans LA	2
Total for 1985	165

APPENDIX B

**Long-Range-Plan Application Capacity and Requirements Data Preparation
Form
(abbreviated form)**

The data documenting the application described in these forms represents descriptive information and estimates available on this application as of January _____, 19__. This data has been augmented by assumptions, as needed, to provide sufficient input for subsequent planning analysis.

Application Name (Acronym): _____

Application Operational Description
Type: Data Entry _____ Information Retrieval _____ Interactive _____
     Remote Batch _____ Other (Specify) _____
User: _____ Office Location: _____
Usage Time: 8 hrs/day _____ more than 8 hrs/day _____ 5 days/week _____
     more than 5 days/week _____ Other (specify) _____

Current Status: Planned _____ Under Development _____ Operational _____
     Expected or Possible Implementation Date: Month _____ Year _____

Hardware
Terminal Type: TTY—CRT _____ IBM 3270 Equivalent _____ Teletypewriter _____
     RJE _____ Other (specify) _____
     Shared _____ hrs/day _____ Nonshared _____
     Locations _____
     Number of Locations (% of Offices) _____

Software
System: IBM 370 _____ Other (specify) _____
Programming Language: COBOL _____ FORTRAN _____ RPG _____
     ALC _____ Pascal _____ Other (specify) _____
System Software: CICS _____ IMS _____ M204 _____ Other (specify) _____

Information Volume
Operator Transaction Inputs per Hour: _____
Transaction: INPUTS   Number of Pages (Screens) _____ Avg. Characters per Page _____
     OUTPUTS Number of Pages (Screens) _____ Avg. Characters per Page _____

Data Base Files
Index Files:
    Name/Function _____ Number of Entries _____ Entry Size _____
    Name/Function _____ Number of Entries _____ Entry Size _____
    Name/Function _____ Number of Entries _____ Entry Size _____

Working Files
    Name/Function _____ Number of Entries _____ Entry Size _____
    Name/Function _____ Number of Entries _____ Entry Size _____
    Name/Function _____ Number of Entries _____ Entry Size _____

Other Resources
Will added user manpower be needed? Yes _____ No _____
How many personnel? _____
Does this increase the office space required? Yes _____ No _____
How many man-months of effort should be expended to develop the software? _____ man-months effort over _____ months
Is formal user training required? Yes _____ No _____

4 Applications of Data Communications Protocol Standards
by James W. Conard

INTRODUCTION

Although data communications protocols offer a wealth of benefits, achieving such benefits is far more difficult than simply obtaining a copy of the appropriate standard and turning it over to designers and implementors. Today, there are more than 100 standards published by recognized standards organizations that relate directly to data communications; and new standards designed to take advantage of rapid technological development continually appear, as is evident in the recent standards for interfacing integrated-circuit modems, public data networks, and local area networks.

The data communications manager can feel overwhelmed by such activity, facing the problem of finding a way through the maze of standards and seeking the knowledge and perspective required before the benefit of proper application of the standards can be realized. This chapter discusses the application of protocol standards at the various architectural levels and the interrelationships and compatibility among the standards, offering practical advice on their choice and specification.

Historical Perspective

The need for standards has been recognized throughout recorded history, probably since man first realized that if two people were going to chisel wheels, it would help if both wheels were of the same diameter. Perhaps the first formal recognition came in 1215 with the inclusion of a chapter on standards in the Magna Carta. Another milestone was a section in the United States Constitution that authorized Congress to establish standards. Standards have been written about everything from abbreviations to zippers, and one current standards catalog contains more than 9,000 entries. During the last two decades, the requirement for standards has grown along with the phenomenal complexity of our technological society.

Early Organizations. Probably the earliest recognition of the need for data communications standards was the founding, in 1865, of the International Telecommunications Union (ITU). The early part of this century saw the

formation of many of the now-familiar organizations: the National Bureau of
Standards (NBS), 1901; American National Standards Institute (ANSI), 1918;
Electronic Industries Association (EIA), 1924; and International Organization
for Standardization (ISO), 1926.

The advent of computer technology and its related communications fostered
the need for standards activity in these disciplines. ITU chartered the International Telegraph and Telephone Consultative Committee (CCITT) in 1957.
ANSI founded the X3 Committee on Computers and Information Processing in
1961, the same year that ISO formed a parallel activity, TC 97, and the
European Computer Manufacturing Association (ECMA) was formed.

These organizations are all deeply involved in data communications and
network standards. Table 4-1 summarizes their membership and data communications responsibilities. During the 1960s, these organizations promulgated
standards that have proved to be of immense value, with such widely known
and implemented standards as EIA RS-232C, the CCITT V series, and the
ANSI character-oriented link control. The past decade has seen an explosive
growth in new standards to match the latest technology. Major developments
include the emergence of bit-oriented link protocols (e.g., HDLC and
ADCCP), the advent of standards for interfacing public packet-switched networks (e.g., X.25), and the more recent activity related to local area networks.

Table 4-1. Major Standards Organizations

Organization	Membership	Responsible Committee for Data Communications	Typical Standards
ANSI	Trade organizations, businesses, government	X3 S3	X3.66 ADCCP
EIA	Electronic manufacturing companies	TR 30	RS-232C RS-449 RS-423
ECMA	European manufacturers	TC 9	ECMA-40, HDLC
CCITT	Public and private telephone companies, scientific organizations	Various study groups	V and X Series
ISO	National standards bodies (e.g., ANSI), liaison members	TC 97 SC6 TC 97 SC16	HDLC, OSI Reference Model

The Standards Dilemma

How does this information make the data communications manager's job
easier? The answer is a good-news/bad-news dilemma.

The Good News. The good news is that communications standards can
potentially provide many kinds of tangible benefits to the data communications
manager. They can:
- Reduce system or network development time by providing knowledge of
  requirements

- Ease procurement problems with commonly available equipment that conforms to standards
- Enhance the marketability of products and services that meet recognized interface standards
- Shorten system checkout, debugging, and installation time because a defined performance baseline exists
- Enhance maintainability by providing inherently compatible test devices

The Bad News. The bad news is that as valuable as standards can be, their proper application places a burden on the data communications manager, whose first objective is to satisfy user requirements in a timely, cost-effective manner. Users are rarely interested in whether RS-232C or V.11 is used as a standard. They are interested only in data actually delivered to an application program or a terminal. The manager, then, must carefully examine the application requirements, map them against the many available standards, and ask:

- Which group of communications standards is applicable to my problem?
- Which specific standard is best suited to my application?
- To what degree are apparently similar standards compatible?
- Can the standard be translated directly to an implementation?
- What must I be aware of when dealing with suppliers?

The following sections of this chapter will attempt to answer these questions.

ARCHITECTURAL MODEL

One approach to the problem of mapping requirements against available protocol standards is to divide the total communications problem into manageable segments. This is one of the purposes of a network architecture. A communications network architecture is simply a formalized logical structure of the interactions and functions necessary to provide the communications services that allow the interchange of information among cooperating processing systems.

Typically, such an architecture is composed of a series of hierarchical layers, each of which provides defined functions related to communications services. This structure is commonly used because it enables the functions and services of one layer to be isolated from another. The task of description, design, and implementation is thus made much simpler.

Development of the ISO Reference Model

The tremendous growth of communications networks, caused primarily by the demands of distributed processing, was leading to a situation that paralleled the early chaotic development of link protocols. Each manufacturer was developing its own method of interconnecting its own products. Each method was, in general, incompatible with others—and was called a network architecture. Examples of these include Burroughs' Network Architecture (BNA), Digital Equipment's Digital Network Architecture (DNA), IBM's System Network Architecture (SNA), and NCR's Distributed Network Architecture (DNA).

This proliferation of architectures, each admirably suited to a specific manufacturer's view of the networking problem, demonstrated a need for a unified approach that would accommodate the interconnection of heterogeneous systems. Such an architecture would permit a system to be open to all other systems complying with the rules of the architecture. Efforts to develop such an architecture have resulted in the hierarchical structure known as *ISO DP7498 Reference Model for Open Systems Interconnection (OSI)*. This model is now in the approval process as an international standard.

The model conceives the communications network as a number of entities connected by some physical medium. Each entity is composed of a logical series of successive layers, as illustrated in Figure 4-1. Each layer performs the functions necessary to provide a defined set of services to the layer above and requests services from the layer below. Because a layer effectively isolates the upper layers from the implementation details of the lower layers, the characteristics of a layer can be changed without affecting the rest of the model (given that the services provided and requested do not change). A character-oriented protocol, for example, could be replaced by a bit-oriented protocol.

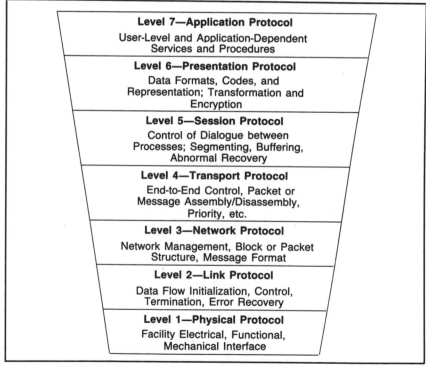

Figure 4-1. Communications Control Hierarchy

Each layer interfaces with the layers above and below it. Data, service requests, and other parameters and control information cross these interfaces.

There are also peer-to-peer protocol relationships with corresponding layers in a connected system or an intermediate network node (if required). These relationships are shown in Figure 4-2; the four lower layers are usually the realm of the data communications manager.

As the name implies, the reference model is not a recommendation for a specific solution to any particular networking problem. It is, instead, an organized means of segmenting and codifying communications functions in a universally applicable manner that has already found wide industry acceptance. (Standards bodies throughout the world are currently generating standards for each of the levels.) The model is thus an immensely valuable tool for the data communications manager, providing an organized approach to resolving the standards dilemma, as discussed in the following sections.

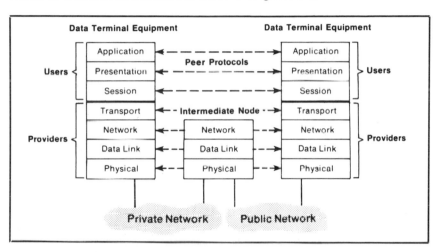

Figure 4-2. Architectural Layers

PHYSICAL INTERFACE PROTOCOLS

The physical layer is the residence of the protocols that define the function and mechanical and electrical characteristics of the interface to the communications medium.

The number of protocols, and, consequently, the number of interface standards, at this layer has kept pace with developments in technology. A decade ago, the data communications manager had to choose between using a current loop and an RS-232C voltage interface. Today, he or she must contend with a wide range of protocol standards. (CCITT and EIA are the major organizations promulgating physical layer standards.) One way to classify the many available interface standards is by application.

General-Purpose Applications

This category includes most of the existing applications that cover relatively simple point-to-point and multipoint private-network configurations, operating (asynchronously or synchronously) at data rates less than 20K bits per second. These standards were designed to match the discrete component technology of the 1960s. If an application calls for interfacing or adding to an existing private network, the following standards may have to be accommodated:

- EIA RS-232C—This is one of the most successful standards ever issued. It describes the interface between data terminal equipment and data communications equipment (a data set or modem) employing serial binary interchange. The latest version was published in 1969.
- CCITT V.24—This standard ("recommendation" in CCITT terminology) actually contains the definitions of the functions for interchange circuits between data terminal and data communications equipment. It does not include specification of electrical characteristics. (These are defined in V.28.)
- CCITT V.28—This recommendation contains the electrical characteristics most often referred to in V.24; its electrical characteristics are compatible with those of RS-232C.
- CCITT V.xx—CCITT usually defines procedural characteristics in a separate recommendation. Such a recommendation would define the modem for a particular class or speed of service (e.g., V.26 for 2,400-bit-per-second operation on leased lines and V.29 for 9,600 bits per second on leased lines.
- ISO IS 2110—The mechanical characteristics of the 25-pin connector and the pin assignments for the interchange circuits are defined in this international standard.

Figure 4-3 summarizes these standards and indicates general compatibility. Note that standards appearing in the same row are compatible but not necessarily identical. V.24, for example, defines many more functional circuits than are used in RS-232C. The federal standards, however, are exact equivalents of their EIA counterparts. It should also be noted that CCITT requires four standards to define an interface completely: the functional definition (e.g., V.24), the procedural subset used by a particular modem (e.g., V.26), a connector (e.g., IS 2110), and the electrical characteristics (e.g., V.28). Because most vendors simply identify their interfaces as RS-232C/V.24 compatible, it is prudent to be careful in this area.

New Technology Applications

The growth of applications requiring longer distances and higher data rates led to a new generation of interface standards. These take advantage of advances in integrated-circuit technology, and the following standards should be applicable to new applications:

- EIA RS-449—This is the parent of a family of standards designed to replace the venerable RS-232C; it defines mechanical and functional characteristics. The standard uses a 37-pin connector in lieu of RS-232C's 25-pin connector. The rest of the RS-449 family includes two standards for electrical characteristics.
- EIA RS-422A—This member of the RS-449 family specifies the electri-

cal characteristics of the balanced-voltage digital interface typical of integrated-circuit implementations. It allows interchange at rates up to 100K bits per second over distances of 4,000 feet and up to 10M bits per second for short distances.

- EIA RS-423—This recommendation specifies the electrical characteristics of unbalanced-voltage interface circuits in the RS-449 family; it interoperates with RS-232C.
- CCITT V.10—This is the CCITT equivalent of RS-423A; it will interoperate, within limits, with CCITT V.28.
- CCITT V.11—This is the equivalent of RS-422A.
- ISO IS 4902—The 37-pin connector used with the newer standards is specified in this international standard. An auxiliary 9-pin connector is also specified for applications that require a secondary channel.

The 37-pin connector and the assignment of single functions per interchange lead constitute a major issue that is delaying adoption of the new standards. Some people argue that technology has surpassed these protocols and the industry should adopt an approach that encodes control functions on a single lead. Such an approach would allow the use of a 15- or even a 9-pin connector.

Application	Protocol	CCITT	EIA	Federal Standard
Synchronous or asynchronous, up to 20K bps. pre-integrated-circuit technology	Functional	V.24 & V.xx	RS-232C	RS-232C
	Mechanical	IS 2110		
	Electrical	V.28		
Synchronous or asynchronous IC Technology	Functional	V.24 & V.xx	RS-449	1031
	Mechanical	IS 4902		
	Electrical, up to 20K bps	V.10	RS-423A	1020A
	Electrical, More than 20K bps	V.11	RS-422A	1030A

Figure 4-3. General-Purpose Interface Standards

Public Data Network Applications

The advent of public data networks, based on packet-switching techniques, spawned a set of protocol standards to interface these networks. The electrical characteristics of the new technology standards described earlier were adopted, and functional protocols appropriate to public data networks were added. Only CCITT has issued recommendations in this category (the X series), but current activity in ANSI and EIA will shortly lead to American standards. Applications that require interfacing a public data network will encounter the following standards for the physical layer:

- CCITT X.20—This recommendation accommodates start-stop character-oriented data terminal equipment interfacing a public data network. All control signaling is in-band, using prescribed characters.

The standard describes the character sequences necessary to establish a circuit, transfer data, and terminate the circuit.

- CCITT X.21—Synchronous equipment interfacing a public data network will probably require this interface. Some networks may allow X.21 bis, as described later. X.21 defines a three-level architecture that includes interchange circuits as well as the character-oriented elements to set up and terminate circuits.
- CCITT X.26—This standard, defining the electrical characteristics for unbalanced interchange circuits, is the exact equivalent of CCITT V.10.
- CCITT X.27—This standard defines the electrical characteristics of balanced interchange circuits; it is the exact equivalent of CCITT V.11.
- ISO IS 4903—This international standard specifies the 15-pin connector and pin assignments widely used in public data networks.

The CCITT also defined methods (the so-called V series) to accommodate the vast amount of existing equipment already in service that might interface with public data networks. This involves two additional standards: the CCITT X.21 bis, the equivalent of EIA RS-232C, and the CCITT V.35, the recommended standard for transmission rates of 48K bits per second. The electrical characteristics are balanced on the data and timing leads and unbalanced (V.28) on the control leads.

The public data network interfaces are summarized in Table 4-2, which indicates that standards shown in the same row are compatible.

Table 4-2. Public Data Network Interface Standards

Application	Protocol	CCITT
V Series Data Terminal Equipment	Functional	X.21 *bis*
	Mechanical, up to 48K bps	IS 2110
	Electrical, up to 48K bps	V.28
	Mechanical, 48K bps	IS 2593
	Electrical, 48K bps	V.35
X Series Data Terminal Equipment	Functional Synchronous	X.21
	Functional Asynchronous	X.20
	Mechanical	IS 4903
	Electrical, up to 9.6K bps	X.26
	Electrical, more than 9.6K bps	X.27

Special-Purpose Applications

This group includes interface requirements, such as the de facto standards used by the Bell System and the military, which are not covered by the standards previously discussed.

Bell System. Most Bell System data sets and systems are compatible with RS-232C; the new sets are compatible with RS-449. One frequently encountered exception is the wideband 303-type interface used for 19.2K to 460.8K bits per second. Others include the wideband 306 interface to T-1 carrier facilities and 1.544-megabit digital service. (There are no EIA equivalent standards for these.) The requirements are defined in the *Bell System Technical References*.

Military Standards. Predominant military standards include Mil-Std-188C, 188-100, and 188-114. These are, in general, compatible with EIA RS-232C and RS-423. One important exception, however, is the propensity of the military standards to reverse the signal sense so that a positive rather than a negative mark is specified.

The physical interface protocols are probably the best defined and most widely understood of all architectural layers. The standards usually contain sufficient detail to allow their use directly as specifications once an application class is chosen, and many of the interfaces are now available in integrated-circuit packages.

DATA LINK PROTOCOLS

Protocols at Layer 2 of the hierarchical structure have evolved from simple, asynchronous, uncontrolled protocols through the character-oriented link controls and their many derivatives to the current bit-oriented link control protocols. The data link protocol is responsible for the initialization, data interchange control, and termination of a link, using a circuit established at the lower level. Perhaps its most important task is recovery from abnormal conditions that occur on the link.

Character-oriented protocols have been characterized by the use of a common code set for both data and control functions. This led to the mixing of link, device, and message control and to the requirement for complicated escape mechanisms to achieve transparency. Although these protocols are, and will remain, in widespread use, their deficiencies have led to the development of bit-oriented protocols, which use fields instead of characters for link control. The entire character set is thus freed for data, and the protocols are naturally code transparent.

Bit-oriented protocols are now coming into widespread use and are the obvious choice for new system development. The major protocol standards of concern are:

- ANSI—Advanced Data Communication Control Procedure (ADCCP), described in X3.66
- ISO—High-Level Data Link Control (HDLC), described in IS 3309, 4335, et al
- CCITT—Link Access Procedure (LAPB), described as Level 2 of Recommendation X.25
- ECMA—High-Level Data Link Control (HDLC), described in ECMA Standard 40

In addition to these, all major vendors as well as the federal government now provide equivalent standards. These bit-oriented standards are all fundamentally compatible. The choices that must be made by the data communications manager are described in the following paragraphs.

Classes of Procedure

Bit-oriented protocol standards have identified classes of procedure that are intended to satisfy the requirements of particular applications. In addition, a number of options may be chosen to refine the protocol for a specific application.

Unbalanced Classes. Control of the data link in this class is unbalanced in favor of the primary control station. This control station carries complete responsibility for link setup, data flow, and error recovery. Secondary stations respond to commands issued by a primary station, and the stations are therefore logically unequal. Unbalanced classes are suitable for point-to-point or multipoint configurations in which centralized control is desirable—for example, a host processor with a family of two-way alternate terminals.

These classes include unbalanced asynchronous (UA) and unbalanced normal (UN). Note that the asynchronous class has nothing to do with the synchronousness of the communications facility, referring instead to a response mode in which the secondary station does not require explicit permission to initiate transmission once the link is active. UA is thus a much less disciplined control than is the normal class, in which a secondary can initiate transmission only after having received explicit permission to do so.

The UN class is ideal for polled multipoint applications requiring orderly interaction between a central control station and remote terminals. The UA class is best suited to situations in which a central control and a single activated remote station wish to exchange data without incurring the overhead penalty of polling. This is usually more efficient in a point-to-point configuration.

Balanced Asynchronous (BA) Class. This class is directed at point-to-point communications between logical equals. Both stations in this arrangement are called combined stations, containing the attributes of primary as well as secondary stations. Each combined station is capable of initializing the data link and is responsible for its own data flow and error recovery. The asynchronous nature of this class means that no polling overhead is required to start or stop data transfer. Balanced operation is best applied in computer-to-computer situations that require two-way simultaneous, efficient, high-speed data transfer. This class also finds application in host-to-network-node and host-to-intelligent-terminal configurations.

Each basic class thus identifies a set of elements, including commands, responses, and a sequence number modulus common to that class. Equipment operating in a given class must implement all of these basic elements.

Options

The bit-oriented protocols also define a set of options that add capability to a basic class or restrict the use of a function. These options are aimed at specific requirements.

Option 1 adds the capability, on a switched network, for exchange identification (XID) commands and responses; it is used to interchange "I am..., who are you?" information.

Two-way simultaneous operation can be enhanced with Option 2, which permits more timely error recovery via the introduction of a reject (REJ) capability.

Option 3 permits a single frame to be selectively rejected (SREJ); it is useful for satellite configurations, along with Option 10, which extends the sequence numbering from 8 to 128.

Downline loading or information related to initializing a remote station would call for Option 5, which adds set and request initialization mode (SIM, RIM) capability. Option 4, unnumbered information, can also be useful in these applications since it permits the transfer of information outside the protection of sequence-number checking.

A requirement to solicit responses from one or more remote stations on a one-time basis can be satisfied by selecting the unnumbered poll (UP), Option 6.

An application requiring more than the 128 addresses permitted by the basic address structure may wish to utilize the extended addressing capability provided by Option 7.

Options 8 and 9 permit information frames to flow in one direction only (e.g., going to a printer or coming from a card reader).

Mode reset, Option 11, is useful in balanced operation when it may be desirable to reset the data link parameters in one direction only rather than reset the entire two-way exchange.

A complete class of procedure is identified by the basic class plus selected options. Class BA28, for example, specifies the balanced class with options for adding the reject command and sending information frames in one direction only. (This is the class used at the Level 2 link access procedure of CCITT X.25.)

A high degree of compatibility exists among the bit-oriented protocols. Since many parameters must be defined, however, the choice involves more than classes of procedure; it encompasses definition of information content, data-field length, addresses, and other parameters. The standards, therefore, should not be used as implementation specifications, although they can be used as a baseline to generate such a specification.

NETWORK PROTOCOLS

The predominant Layer 3 protocol by far is CCITT X.25. Although data communications managers will have no trouble finding X.25-compatible equipment and services, they must be careful to define what they mean by "compatible"—there are many problems associated with this word.

Architecture

The first problem is that of architecture. X.25 spans the three lowest layers of the OSI reference model, making direct reference to X.21 at the physical layer. (X.21 bis, the equivalent of RS-232C, is permitted for an interim period by some networks.) It is important to determine exactly which interface an X.25 network vendor accommodates.

Services

Another issue is that of services. X.25 offers three distinct services from which a choice must be made, depending on the application:
- Virtual call service is somewhat analogous to dial-up service in that a connection must be established and terminated for each exchange, using appropriate packets.
- A permanent virtual circuit behaves much like a dedicated line and eliminates the overhead associated with virtual call service.
- Datagram service provides a method of sending single independent packets without any notion of a connection existing between sender and receiver.

Many options and issues for further study exist in X.25. More than 23 optional user facilities are defined indirectly in X.25 and are actually listed in X.2. These cover areas from extended packet-sequence numbering to selection of closed user groups. The data communications manager must make appropriate choices and be prepared to resolve issues that are earmarked for further study ("for further study" cannot be implemented). Most vendors will have taken a position on such issues, but the positions of any two vendors may not be compatible.

Link Access Procedures

Another area of concern is link access procedures—LAP and LAPB. As originally defined, the X.25 data-link access procedure was not compatible with the bit-oriented procedure standardized by ISO under HDLC. This shortcoming was corrected with the newer LAPB link access procedure balanced, which differs slightly from LAP and is compatible with HDLC Class BA28 (as described earlier). Although both LAP and LAPB will be available for an interim period, the latter will eventually be the only access procedure offered by all networks.

Packet Assembler-Disassembler Functions

An application that calls for interfacing a start-stop terminal to a public data network requires dealing with a different set of X.25-related standards that define packet assembler-disassembler (PAD) functions. A PAD transforms the data flowing from a start-stop terminal into the protocol required by the public network. PAD standards include:

- CCITT X.3—This recommendation describes the PAD functions and the control protocol necessary to convert serial data from the start-stop terminal into packet format for the network.
- CCITT X.28—This is the protocol for operation of a simple start-stop terminal connected to a PAD.
- CCITT X.29—This standard identifies the procedures to be used by X.25 equipment to control the PAD through a public network when the PAD is connected to an X.28 terminal.

Point of View

A final network issue deals with the point of view taken by the standards. Although CCITT standards predominate at this layer, it is important to remember that CCITT describes the behavior of the network rather than that of the equipment connected to it. Implementing CCITT standards directly in data terminal equipment connected to a network can cause difficulties, since the behavior is not precisely symmetrical. ANSI and some vendors, however, are now generating network interface standards from the equipment point of view.

Network layer protocols require precise specification, using the standards as a baseline. Direct implementation of the standard, without analysis, could cause difficulty and might well be disastrous. Most network vendors therefore provide (for a fee) a testing service to check equipment and software prior to actual operation on the network.

TRANSPORT PROTOCOLS

Layer 4 of the reference model forms the upper boundary of the services usually considered the province of the communicators. It also represents that amorphous boundary between data communications and data processing. (There is even some controversy over the division of functions between the third and fourth layers.) For these reasons, the process of formalizing standards at the transport level is just now beginning.

Transport protocols are intended to provide network-independent end-to-end transport of data between connected systems. The transport protocol could, for example, save costs by supporting the multiplexing of several applications or sessions on a single network connection. These protocols will also be heavily concerned with connection reliability and service quality.

User Services. There will undoubtedly be a family of protocols at the transport level to provide various user classes of service. These protocols will range from very simple to very powerful and will include multiplexing, seg-menting, high-level flow control, and complete fault recovery. (The Depart-ment of Defense Transport Control Protocol TCP-4 is an example of a very powerful protocol.) All of the standards organizations are working on transport layer standard protocols; an ambitious National Bureau of Standards program is aimed at developing standards at higher levels of the architecture. For the moment, however, data communications managers can only carefully follow and, if possible, urge their organizations to participate in the development process.

LOCAL AREA NETWORKS

No discussion of current communications protocol standards would be complete without at least a mention of local area networks. Data communica-tions managers have traditionally linked computational resources by using long-haul facilities provided by common carriers. Even for only local distribu-tion (e.g., a campus environment), interconnection often required the use of relatively expensive common-carrier facilities and equipment to translate digi-tal data to analog form for transmission over such conventional facilities.

The increasing requirement for sharing distributed resources in industrial and automated-office applications provided an additional impetus for develop-ment of the distributed communications techniques now known as local area networks.

The first problem faced by a manager seeking to take advantage of this technology is that of definition. There is still no universally accepted definition of what constitutes a local area network. There does seem to be general agreement that a local area network involves distances of less than 10 kilome-ters at data rates up to 20 megabits per second. Such networks can be further characterized as using inexpensive media (e.g., coaxial cable) and having high connectivity and no centralized control.

Two major standards activities are pressing toward local area network protocol standards. The Process Highway (PROWAY)/Purdue Workshop ac-tivity, under the auspices of the International Electrotechnical Commission, is focused primarily on industrial applications. The Local Area Network Com-mittee, working under the IEEE Computer Society, is seeking a general solution. In addition, many industrial organizations are actively pursuing standards and network development. The most prominent of these is the Digital Equipment, INTEL, and Xerox arrangement, which is promoting the Ethernet approach.

Although there are many differences in the approaches to local area network standards, most share certain characteristics. They all use bus topology, source and destination addresses, a layered approach to architecture (more or less compatible with OSI), coaxial-cable-type media, and high-order error-protection schemes.

Many controversial issues must also be resolved: details of the link layer protocols, other media types, network gateways, and (especially) media access strategies. It is likely that several standards will be published with differing access methods and protocols. Data communications managers contemplating a local area network must, therefore, be very thorough and cautious in mapping requirements against the features offered.

CONCLUSION

Communications protocol standards can prove extremely useful to both managers and users of data communications systems. Interaction among the standards organizations is leading to a high level of compatibility between related standards, and the OSI reference model disciplines the standards-making process by providing a basic framework for such construction.

Despite the global acceptance of standards and the tendency of manufacturers to describe their products as compatible, the standards alone cannot be substituted for specifications. They should be used as a base on which to build a definitive specification for an implementation. This specification will choose options, detail system parameters, and, in general, flesh out the skeleton presented by the standard.

A data communications manager, whether involved in private, public, or local networking as an implementor or a user, can be well served by compatible protocol standards. Each application must be partitioned into manageable segments, and the applicable standards must be chosen and prudently applied. The result will be a smoothly integrated, cost-effective, and reliable data communications system.

5 The RS-449 Interface

by Richard Parkinson

INTRODUCTION

A key component in any data communications network is the interface that connects data terminal equipment (DTE) to data circuit-terminating equipment (DCE). Although the Electronic Industries Association (EIA) RS-232C interface standard has served the industry well and is still widely used, the demands of new applications have exceeded its capacity. Fortunately, a relatively new standard, EIA RS-449, is gaining momentum and seems destined to replace RS-232C. This chapter discusses the evolution and capabilities of this new interface, its compatibilities with other standards, and its future.

The EIA

EIA is an association of electronic equipment manufacturers in the United States; the association is also a member of the American National Standards Institute (ANSI). An EIA subcommittee is responsible for interface compatibility, enhancing existing standards, and/or developing new standards. Working papers are developed by committee members, with several iterations that include input from outside interested parties; a final draft is voted on by the EIA general committee. This was the procedure followed in the development of RS-449 and its companion standards, RS-422 and RS-423.

Defining an Interface

The interface discussed here connects a DTE (a terminal device or computer) to a DCE (a traditional digital-to-analog modem or line driver [a digital-to-digital device]). Figure 5-1 shows these two components joined by a multi-wire cable. Each wire lead passes low-voltage electrical signals between the two devices, with the direction of flow (to or from the DCE) specified by the EIA standard. Each wire is assigned one of four basic functions:
- Data transfer
- Control signals
- Timing
- Signal grounds

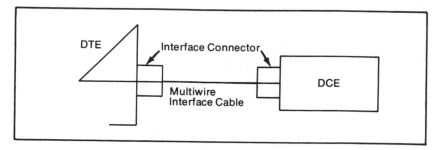

Figure 5-1. Joining a DTE and a DCE

Both RS-449 and its predecessor, RS-232C, perform these basic functions over wires that conveniently terminate in a connector that joins the DTE and DCE. Thus, the three components of an interface are functional information transmitted by electrical signals over wires that terminate in a mechanical connector.

EVOLUTION OF THE INTERFACE

RS-232C was (and still is) the most predominant DTE/DCE interface standard since the early 1960s. Improved technology and application demands, however, have exceeded the interface's capabilities (a fact that was recognized in the early 1970s). In today's environment, RS-232C carries such deficiencies as:

- A maximum DTE-to-DCE signaling rate of 20,000 bits per second.
- A maximum distance between DTE and DCE of, nominally, 50 cable feet; in practice, with shielded cable, a distance of several hundred feet is possible.
- Some manufacturers arbitrarily assign features not supported by RS-232C to any unused pin.
- Because RS-232C did not specify any particular mechanical interface connector, many different and incompatible designs proliferated; some connectors, for example, were attached to the DTE with screws and others with clips.

Because the first two points on this list were the most troublesome, these areas were addressed first. The results were the RS-422 standard for balanced circuits and the RS-423 for unbalanced circuits, both of which were issued in 1975. Although detailed electrical engineering information on the differences is beyond the scope of this chapter, it is available in the standards documents (see Suggested Readings). The following information, however, should be sufficient to understand why RS-422 and RS-423 provide better performance characteristics than RS-232C. Figure 5-2 shows the three approaches to electrical signaling between a DTE and a DCE. With RS-232C, both the generator and receiver circuitry share a common ground wire in both directions (pin 7, signal ground). Sharing a common ground reduces the immunity to the noise caused by one circuit's signals interacting with the signals of another. (This phenomenon manifests itself in an automobile tape deck or radio as a high-

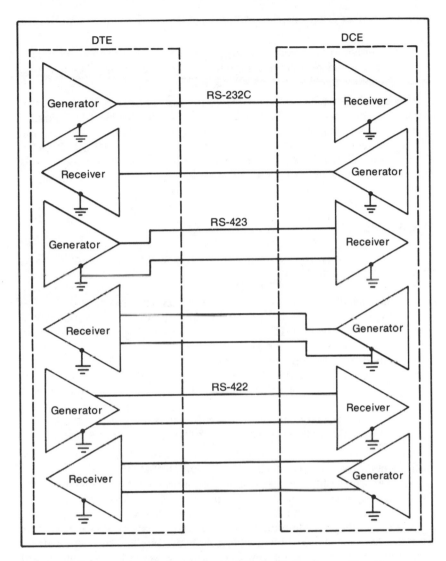

Figure 5-2. Balanced versus Unbalanced Interchange Circuits

pitched whine that varies with engine revolutions per minute. In this example, the radio ground is not isolated from other signal grounds and causes the interference.) This common ground, more than any other, is the factor that limits speed and distance when using RS-232C.

RS-423 provides for unbalanced electrical characteristics where the generator at either end shares a common ground, but the RS-423 receivers have separate grounds. The primary application of RS-423 is to provide compatibility with RS-232C when a DTE or DCE has the opposite interface to its connected partner. This allows transition from RS-232C equipment to RS-449 as needed.

RS-422 provides balanced electrical characteristics where both generator and receiver use independent ground wires. This isolation of grounds allows greater capability than does RS-232C or RS-423.

Although the RS-232C standard covers the functional, electrical, and mechanical components, RS-422 and RS-423 address only the electrical requirements. A new standard was therefore needed to cover the functional and mechanical requirements. That standard, issued by EIA in 1977, is RS-449. The remainder of this chapter deals primarily with the functional aspects of this relatively new standard that are of primary interest to data communications users.

THE STANDARD

Of the advantages offered by the RS-449 standard over its predecessor, RS-232C, the most notable are:

- Signaling rates over the DTE/DCE interface of up to 2M bits per second (see Table 5-1), which is considered a conservative practical speed. For shorter distances, the full RS-422 signaling limits would be applicable.
- A distance between DTE and DCE of up to 4,000 feet at approximately 100K bits per second (see Table 5-1).
- Addition of 10 new circuit functions.
- Elimination of three RS-232C circuits.
- Segregation of secondary-channel circuits into a separate 9-pin connector.
- Use by the primary circuits of a new 37-pin connector (the mechanical characteristics of these two connectors form part of the standard).

It is essential that users understand the capabilities of RS-449, both to ensure its efficient utilization and to diagnose problems attributable to either the DTE or the DCE. Appendixes A and B contain equivalency tables that show the functional assignments of the pins for both RS-232C and RS-449. For clarity, the comparison is based on the four duties of these leads (i.e., grounds, data, control, and timing). In the primary channel equivalency table (see Appendix A), it should be noted that some functions show two pins assigned while others show only one. Functions with only one pin are referred to as Category II

Table 5-1. Comparison of Distance versus Data Signaling Rate

Distance (ft)	RS-232C	RS-423	RS-422
10	≥ 20K bps	> 100K bps	10M bps
40	≥ 20K bps	100K bps	10M bps
50	20K bps	≅ 90K bps	≅ 9M bps
100	< 20K bps	≅ 80K bps	≅ 5M bps
1,000	NA	≅ 6K bps	≅ 500K bps
4,000	NA	≅ 900 bps	≅ 100K bps

circuits; those with two pin assignments are called Category I circuits. The latter are used for data signaling and control functions that must respond very rapidly at high data rates. Category II circuits are those that are not required to change their state quickly, so sharing a common ground is quite adequate.

Appendix C compares pin assignments of RS-449 and RS-232C and provides a brief functional description of each RS-449 interface lead. (There is a great deal of similarity with RS-232C functions; some have new names but perform the same job.) One improvement provided by RS-449 is the designation of mnemonics that more closely relate to the actual functions. "Clear to send," for example, was given the mnemonic CB with RS-232C; with RS-449 it is CS. In practice, however, the more common mnemonic for clear to send has been CTS, and it is doubtful that the advent of RS-449 will quickly persuade users to move from CTS to CS.

RS-449 also provides more substantive features in addition to improved speed and distance. Most of these new functions are service oriented, allowing testing and restoral capabilities under DTE control, as shown in Figure 5-3.

Of particular interest are the select standby (SS) and standby indicator (SB) leads (shown in Figure 5-3a). By turning on the SS lead (pin 32), the DTE instructs the modem to use an alternate standby facility. This would, for

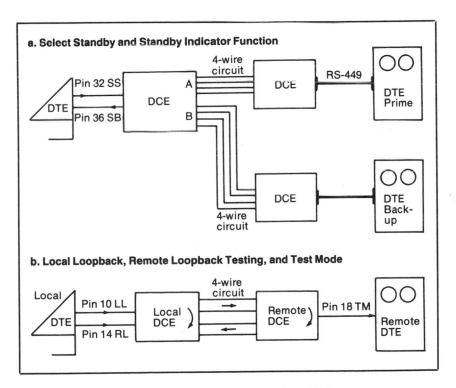

Figure 5-3. Testing and Restoral Capabilities

example, be a change from primary private-line service to packet-switched service either for backup or simply to access another data base not generally used. This eliminates manual patching, switching keys, and so on. The SB lead (pin 36) serves as the DCE's reminder to the DTE that standby facilities are in use.

The DTE can now invoke tests to isolate problems with either the local or remote DCE or the communications line. Figure 5-3b shows the local loopback (LL, pin 10) and the remote loopback (RL, pin 14) testing function. Suitably capable DTEs and DCEs allow these basic tests without requiring test equipment or manual swapping in and out of equipment and cables (local loopback and remote loopback are mutually exclusive tests). Suitably equipped DCEs on a multipoint line could also be selected for testing by the local DTE.

Adding the terminal in service (IS) lead allows the DTE to advise the DCE of its inability to accept data. When used by a DTE in a rotary hunting group, this lead allows the DTE to make the DCE appear in use to the network. The select frequency (SF) lead allows the DTE to choose between a high ("on" condition) or low ("off" condition) frequency for transmission. It could be used, for example, with a full-duplex, 2-wire modem involving both a transmit and a receive frequency. In this case, either end would be able to send or receive, no matter which DTE originated the call.

CCITT X.21 "Mini Interface"

Another point that must be mentioned briefly is the CCITT Recommendation X.21, often referred to as the mini interface. Some industry spokesmen believe that this interface may very quickly replace RS-449. The design is based on fewer wires (only 15) connecting the DTE and DCE; however, this requires increased intelligence in both DTE and DCE, with two wires replacing the many used by RS-449 for control functions. At present, X.21 is not suitable for the analog private lines, switched lines, or half-duplex lines that constitute a considerable majority of existing data communications links. Based on the slow acceptance of RS-449 as a new standard and the fact that there are no known X.21 networks planned in North America, it is reasonable to consider the X.21 interface some years away from practical applications in the U.S. and Canada. It should be noted that during its development, an appendix to RS-449 was added, indicating that the X.21 interface was considered to ensure a maximum degree of compatibility. To this end, there is sufficient commonality between RS-449 and X.21 that a simple connector adapter will allow RS-449 DTEs to connect to X.21 DCEs. Users should thus have a painless transition from RS-449 to X.21.

Equivalent Standards

One of the more confusing aspects of standards is the number of groups involved in setting them. EIA is a domestic association, and its standards are used by equipment manufacturers supplying the U.S. and Canada. Manufacturers wanting to enter the international market must also conform to (for the most part) equivalent standards adopted by the CCITT. The CCITT equivalent standards (recommendations) for RS-449, RS-422, and RS-423 are V.24, V.11, and V.10, respectively. While the circuit names may be different, they are functionally identical. The U.S. federal government has also adopted equivalent standards: FED-STD-1031, FED-STD-1020, and FED-STD-1030, respectively. The purpose of each of these standards is to accommodate unique characteristics if and when appropriate.

Suggested Readings. Readers who wish more detail than that provided in this chapter can obtain the actual standards documents from the EIA. The documents (which were used in preparing this chapter) are comprehensive yet easy to read and understand; they should be required reading for everyone involved in network problems.

RS-232C	"Interface Between Data Terminal Equipment and Data Communications Equipment Employing Serial Binary Data Interchange"
RS-422	"Electrical Characteristics of Balanced Voltage Digital Interface Circuits"
RS-423	"Electrical Characteristics of Unbalanced Voltage Digital Interface Circuits"
RS-449	"General Purpose 37-Position and 9-Position Interface for Data Terminal Equipment and Data Circuit-Terminating Equipment Employing Serial Binary Data Exchange"
Bulletin #9	"Application Notes for EIA Standard RS-232C"
Bulletin #12	"Application Notes on Interconnection Between Interface Circuits Using RS-449 and RS-232C"

All of these documents are available from:

Electronic Industries Association
2001 Eye Street NW
Washington DC 20006
(202) 457-4900

THE FUTURE OF RS-449

Although the enhanced capabilities now available should be incorporated into new product offerings by DTE and DCE manufacturers, adoption of these new features has, sadly, been minimal. Most vendors who now support the RS-449 interface are simply duplicating RS-232C functions, with greater speed and distance as the only tangible benefits. Support for the standard would probably not be as advanced as it is but for the federal government's adoption of the RS-449-equivalent, Fed-Std-1031, which became mandatory for all procurements after June 1, 1980. It is apparent from discussing the future of

RS-449 with marketing personnel of both DCE and DTE vendors that the advantages are not yet well understood. It will therefore benefit users to put pressure on their suppliers to ensure the availability of these new capabilities.

The greatly enhanced data-rate performance (up to 2M bits per second) will allow the development of higher-speed DTEs and DCEs that will be valuable in many applications. A common DTE/DCE interface for all but the very high volume applications will also be possible, simplifying multispeed networks. Greater use by large corporate networks of digital T-1 carrier links operating at 1.544M bits per second will offer data communications users more opportunity to use high-speed links economically, and inexpensive DCEs will allow DTEs access to this high-speed capacity. Since RS-449 now supports this speed, DTE and DCE designers must capitalize on its capabilities.

APPENDIX A

RS-449 and RS-232C Equivalency Table: Primary Channels

RS-449					RS-232C		
	Desig-		Direction			Desig-	
			From	To			
Pin #	nation	Description	DCE	DCE	Pin #	nation	Description
1	NA	Shield	NA	NA	1	AA	Protective ground
19	SG	Signal ground	NA	NA	7	AB	Signal ground
20	RC	Receive common	X				
37	SC	Send common		X			
4/22	SD	Send data		X	2	BA	Transmitted data
6/24	RD	Receive data	X		3	BB	Received data
2	SI	Signaling rate indi-cator	X		23	CH	Data rate selector
3/21	*	Spare	*	*			
7/25	RS	Request to send		X	4	CA	Request to send
9/27	CS	Clear to send	X		5	CB	Clear to send
10	LL	Local loopback		X			
11/29	DM	Data mode	X		6	CC	Data set ready
12/30	TR	Terminal ready		X	20	CD	Data terminal ready
13/31	RR	Receiver ready	X		8	CF	Received line signal detector
14	RL	Remote loopback		X			
15	IC	Incoming call	X		22	CE	Ring indicator
16	SR	Signaling rate		X	23	CH	Data rate selector
16	SF	Select frequency	X				
18	TM	Test mode	X				
28	IS	Terminal in service		X			
32	SS	Select standby		X			
33	SQ	Signal quality	X		21	CG	Signal quality detec-tor
34	NS	New signal		X	11/14		Optionally used for new synchroniza-tion
36	SB	Standby indicator	X				
5/23	ST	Send timing	X		15	DB	Transmitter signal el-ement timing
8/26	RT	Receive timing	X		17	DD	Receiver signal ele-ment timing
17/35	TT	Terminal timing		X	24	DA	Transmitter signal el-ement timing

Notes:
NA Not applicable
*   Reserved for future use

APPENDIX B

RS-449 and RS-232C Equivalency Table: Secondary Channels

| RS-449 | | | Direction | | RS-232C | | |
Pin #	Desig-nation	Description	From DCE	To DCE	Pin #	Desig-nation	Description
1	*	Shield	*	*	1	AA	Protective ground
5	SG	Signal ground	NA	NA	7	AB	Signal ground
6	RC	Receiver common	X				
9	SC	Send common		X			
3	SSD	Secondary send data		X	14	SBA	Secondary transmit data
4	SRD	Secondary receive data	X		16	SBB	Secondary receive data
2	SRR	Secondary receiver ready	X		12	SCF	Secondary receive signal detect
7	SRS	Secondary request to send		X	19	SCA	Secondary request to send
8	SCS	Secondary clear to send	X		13	SCB	Secondary clear to send

Notes:
NA   Not applicable
*   Reserved for future use

APPENDIX C

Function Description of RS-449 Interface Leads

RS-449 Pin #	RS-232C Pin #		
1	1	**Shield ground**	Used to allow tandem sections of shielded cable to retain continuity through the connector
19	7	**Signal ground**	Directly connects the DTE circuit ground to the DCE circuit ground, providing a path for DTE and DCE signal commons
20	NA	**Receive common**	Provides a reference potential from the DCE circuit ground to the DTE for Category II circuit receivers
37	NA	**Send common**	Provides a reference potential from the DTE circuit ground to the DCE for Category II circuit receivers
4/22	2	**Send data**	Used by the DTE to pass binary data to the DCE for transmission over the communications channel
6/24	3	**Receive data**	Used by the DCE to pass binary data received from the communications channel to the DTE

RS-449 Pin #	RS-232C Pin #		
2	23	Signaling rate indicator	For DCEs capable of two data rates; an on condition indicates the higher rate, an off condition signifies the lower rate to the DTE
3/21		Spare	Reserved for future use
7/25	4	Request to send	Used by the DTE to advise the DCE it wishes to transmit data
9/27	5	Clear to send	Used by the DCE to advise the DTE that the DCE is ready to send data over the communications channel
10	NA	Local loopback	Voltage on this lead causes the DCE to isolate the communications channel and to connect the transmit signal converter to the receive signal converter, allowing the DTE to test its local DCE transmit and receive circuitry.
11/29	6	Data mode	Used to advise the DTE of the ready status of the DCE. In most cases, it simply implies the unit is powered on, although in auto-answer mode this lead is usually off when no call is in progress.
12/30	20	Terminal ready	Used by the DTE to advise the DCE it is ready to transmit or receive
13/31	8	Receiver ready	The DCE uses this lead to advise the DTE that an incoming signal on the communications channel is present. When first initialized, it is an indication to the DTE to expect data momentarily.
14	NA	Remote loopback	Causes a local DCE, on receipt of an on condition from the local DTE, to signal the remote DCE to isolate the remote DTE and connect the receive leads to the transmit leads. This allows the local DTE to test both DCEs and the communications channel.
15	22	Incoming call	Allows the DCE, on detecting a ringing signal from the communications line, to advise the DTE of an incoming call
16	23	Signaling rate selector	Allows the DTE, when working with a dual-data-rate DCE, to select the rate: an on condition for the higher rate, an off for the lower rate Note: On some DCEs, this lead will override the manual switch setting on DCE.
16	NA	Select frequency	Allows the DTE to select a higher-frequency band for transmission with an on condition, or a lower-frequency band for transmission with an off condition
18	NA	Test mode	Used by the DCE to advise the DTE whenever it is in test mode.

RS-449 Pin #	RS-232C Pin #		
28	NA	**Terminal in service**	Used by the DTE to advise the DCE whether it is available for service. It is particularly useful in line-hunting applications, allowing the DTE to place itself in an out-of-service condition (i.e., to indicate to the DCE that the DTE is busy).
32	NA	**Select standby**	Allows the DTE to instruct the DCE to select standby facilities (e.g., dial-up backup lines)
33	21	**Signal quality**	Based on the criteria established by the DCE manufacturer in monitoring the quality of the incoming signal to the DCE from the communications line, an on condition will be construed as good data, an off condition as poor data.
34	11/14	**New signal**	Applicable to multipoint links. Because of the lack of clock synchronization on incoming messages from terminal to terminal, clock holdover at the end of one message may impair resynchronization for the next message. The DTE can assist by applying an on condition to the lead recognized by the DCE, which immediately synchronizes to the new signal.
36	NA	**Standby indicator**	Used by the DCE to advise the DTE whenever standby facilities (e.g., dial-up backup) are in use
5/23	15	**Send timing**	Allows the DCE to transmit signal element timing to the DTE. This allows the DTE send data signal on circuit SD to be in synchronization with on/off transitions on this lead.
8/26	17	**Receive timing**	Transitions on this lead allow the DTE to time data received over circuit RD
17/35	24	**Terminal timing**	Allows the DTE to provide transmit timing information to the DCE so that it can synchronize with data arriving over the SD lead

Note:
NA Not applicable

⑥ Introduction to SNA

by Pete Moulton

INTRODUCTION

Although one more revolutionary electronic discovery or component seems to be announced every month, computer and data communications products to use these discoveries evolve at a significantly slower rate. One such set of products is IBM's System Network Architecture (SNA). In the 1960s, IBM's data processing products focused on batch processing, with data communications permitted on a limited scale. IBM offerings at that time included Model 2260 CRT terminals for transaction processing, the Model 2741 teleprinter terminal for time sharing, and the Model 2780 remote batch terminal for remote batch applications. The use of a different communications protocol by each of these terminals made coherent network plans impossible. In addition, significant reprogramming for both system and applications software was required whenever the network configuration changed. IBM terminal products moved toward using a common communications protocol (BSC) following the late-1960s introduction of the Model 3270 terminal. It was still frequently necessary, however, to write programs to control communications lines, accommodate unique terminal-display formatting features, and ensure data accuracy.

In 1974, IBM announced SNA as its comprehensive plan for future data communications networks. The announcement also introduced the synchronous data link control (SDLC) protocol and several communications hardware and software products using it. Three network layers—communications system, transmission subsystem, and common network—were identified initially. A single access method, VTAM, resident in the host computer, and a single network control program, NCP, resident in a front-end communications processor, were offered, along with terminals that used the new SDLC protocol. Although SNA was considered a comprehensive design, IBM at first delivered only the most basic products required for network implementation. The SNA capabilities had been extended by 1976 to permit interconnection of multiple mainframes, using the multisystem networking facility (MSNF), which required changes to the path control layer (the NCP software in the front end). SNA has currently evolved to provide a greater level of insulation between the application programmer and the data communications network, making teleprocessing applications easier to develop and implement. The SNA design objectives have remained constant during this evolution; the design details have been completed and released. The new SNA features and capabilities result mainly from software changes rather than from new hardware components. For example, the network terminal option (NTO) program (run in the 3705-II front-end communications processor) permits the use of start-stop (asynchronous) terminals, easing the transition to SNA networks. (The initial SNA announcement provided little support for such transition.)

Data Communications Network Architecture

A network architecture is a set of specifications and rules that acts as a blueprint for interconnecting all system components—hardware, software, and communications services. It requires communications protocols to permit the transmission of data between network components, commands and responses to provide control mechanisms between and among software and hardware, and the hardware and software necessary for implementation.

Network architectures also provide such key features as the following:
- Layers—The International Standards Organization (ISO) has developed an Open Systems Interconnection (OSI) reference model with seven layers. SNA layers currently correspond fairly closely with the OSI model.
- Logical structure—The logical structure identifies all components by their network addresses. There is a correspondence between the logical structure and the physical network structure.
- End-to-end communications—Architectures provide mechanisms for end-to-end communications regardless of how the data is routed through the physical facilities. Data, commands, and status information can thus be exchanged between any components throughout the network. SNA end-to-end routing mechanisms choose paths based on facility availability, which is determined by traffic load, transmission priority, and desired level of data security. Multiple active routing distributes traffic from several users over the available routes.
- Network control and management facility—Control mechanisms are essential to monitor the use and status of all network components and to allocate network resources to each user requesting service. Such a facility also serves as a central monitoring and trouble-reporting control point for operations personnel. (The operator interface to SNA's control facility, described later in this chapter, is implemented through the network communications control facility program.)

Objectives

Network architectures are designed to fulfill the following objectives:
- Insulate programmers from data communications network concerns. Programmers should not be involved with the details of communications between computer and terminal. They should request communications I/O through macrocommands, and data-routing and error-recovery func-

tions should be performed by the communications software. This will also aid in reducing the effort required by system programmers to implement and reconfigure a network.

- Provide a mechanism to develop and implement complex networks. It should be possible to interconnect multiple mainframe computers as well as remote processors in hierarchical or distributed networks, permitting implementation of distributed DP applications.
- Support generalized applications (e.g., remote batch, inquiry/response, time sharing) and industry-specific applications (e.g., supermarket checkout, financial transaction processing, point-of-sale data acquisition) using the same mainframe hardware and software components. Both specialized and general-purpose terminals can thus be used in the same network.
- Permit network expansion or reconfiguration with minimal disruption of current operations. Network changes should not require reprogramming of applications or reconstruction of the system software in the host. Once a network is operational, changes are performed most effectively by the network operating personnel.
- Provide high levels of network availability and security. Availability requires multiple communications paths to allow switching when outages occur. Security mechanisms should accommodate several levels of risk.
- Use network resources efficiently. Communications channel capacity is often wasted in order to provide adequate peak-period service. Providing time-critical applications (e.g., transaction processing) with a high transmission priority and less time-critical applications (e.g., remote batch) with a lower priority can average the transmission loads and increase utilization of network resources.

Few architectures fulfill all these objectives. For example, only simple centralized networks could initially be constructed from SNA components. MSNF, however, soon allowed development of more complex networks with interconnected IBM/370 mainframes. Today, 370s can be interconnected, and various smaller IBM processors (System/34 or 38, Series 1, or the Model 8100 system) can be incorporated into the network. Thus, although SNA did not fulfill all these objectives at the outset, it has now evolved to meet most of them.

Notably absent from the objectives and key features is the ability to interconnect with other operational networks using other vendors' public data networks (PDNs) and architectures. The design focus to date has been to provide the tools to make teleprocessing application software development easy. These tools will also make operating a large-scale network manageable by helping to isolate, predict (when possible), and bypass equipment and circuit malfunctions and outages. Interconnection and compatibility with other networks, which can lead to replacement of one vendor's products with another vendor's lower-cost components that perform equivalent functions, has not been a design consideration. Therefore, only vendors wishing to replace IBM SNA products with their own have announced such capabilities (and then only with SNA).

Other Manufacturers

Almost every computer manufacturer who offers products designed to implement distributed DP systems has announced the development of a network architecture. (Some manufacturers fit within the SNA umbrella and do not offer separate architectures; a few, such as Control Data Corporation and Cray Research, are in specialized market areas and have seen no need to develop them.) All these architectures were announced (after SNA) in the late 1970s; some have also gone through evolutionary phases.

The following manufacturers (in addition to IBM) currently offer network architectures:
- Sperry Univac—Distributed Communication Architecture (DCA)
- Burroughs—Burroughs Network Architecture (BNA)
- Honeywell—Distributed Systems Architecture
- National Cash Register (NCR)—Distributed Network Architecture
- NCR/Comten—Communications Networking System (CNS)
- Digital Equipment Corporation—DECnet
- Hewlett-Packard—Distributed Systems Network
- Data General—XODIAC
- Prime—Primenet
- Tandem—Guardian/Expand
- Computer Automation—SyFA (System for Automation) Virtual Network
- Datapoint—Attached Resource Computer (ARC)
- Modcomp—MAXNET

In some cases, these offerings are responses to the rhetoric that followed the introduction of SNA, with existing product plans quickly relabeled and marketed as comprehensive network architectures. In other cases, an architecture for data communications applications was offered, but it was not so labeled. An example is the NCR/Comten Communications Networking System, which fits under the IBM umbrella and provides advanced networking features.

Other manufacturers, in concentrating on the problem of reducing the programming effort required to develop telecommunications applications, have, as a result, developed products that provide architectural capabilities. Hewlett-Packard, for example, originally produced software packages to make application program development on their minicomputer products easy to do. These development tools were later expanded to support applications that used more than one computer. HP's architecture is thus more concerned with data communications as an essential ingredient of application programs (with data bases and processing distributed over several minicomputer systems) than with interconnecting computer systems through data communications.

Digital Equipment Corporation's DECnet was similarly developed to assist programmers in constructing application programs that involved geographically dispersed data bases and processing. DECnet, however, uses a single communications protocol between all Digital Equipment products, while HP uses various protocols for computer-to-terminal and network-computer-to-network-computer (network-node) communications. Several other manufacturers also use multiple protocols.

In contrast, when IBM first emphasized SNA's communications capabilities, its ability to ease application program development was nonexistent. IBM has now begun to identify the SNA software packages that are aimed at easing this effort.

System Network Architecture Defined

An SNA network is defined by the hardware and software components comprising it. Figure 6-1 shows SNA hardware and software components in a simplified network configuration. SNA hardware includes:

- Mainframe computers—IBM System/370s, 303xs, and the 43xx series can be used as SNA mainframe computers. They can act as the central

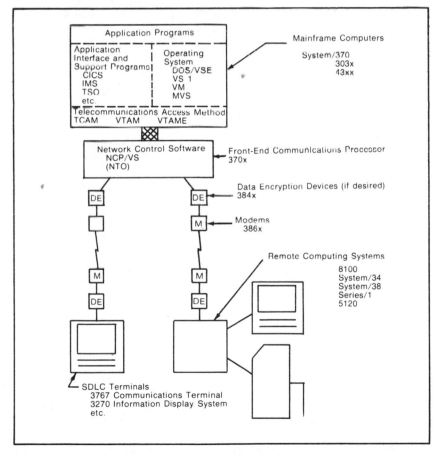

Figure 6-1. SNA Network Components

node for a single network, or they can be interconnected to form fully distributed networks.

- Front-end communications processors—The IBM 3705-II Communications Controller is the processor primarily used for SNA networks: in some cases, an integrated communications adapter can be used instead.
- Data encryption devices—Although not required, IBM 3845 and 3846 data encryption devices can be included to provide increased network security.
- Modems—Three microprocessor-controlled modems operate with IBM programs in both the mainframe and the front end to assist network operators in identifying and isolating malfunctions. The modems are not required for SNA; however, they fit into the SNA structure and provide enhanced features.
- SDLC terminals—More than 10 terminals and terminal systems can be used to implement an SNA network. They range from the 3767 Communications Terminal (teleprinter) to the 3270 Information Display System (standalone or clustered alphanumeric displays with associated printers) through industry-specific terminals, such as the 3660 Supermarket System (a cash register unit with associated scanner). All SNA terminals must use SDLC. (The 3101 is not considered an SNA terminal because it uses only an asynchronous TTY protocol. In contrast, the 3767 is so considered because it supports both SDLC and an asynchronous TTY protocol.)
- Remote computing systems—IBM offers several remote computing systems that can be used as standalone computers or as remote distributed processors under SNA. These systems support both SNA and non-SNA terminals; their interconnection with the IBM mainframe, however, is through an SDLC communications channel.

SNA is IBM's answer to distributed DP requirements, distributing functions from the mainframe to other network components. SNA terminals are therefore assumed to have more intelligence than pre-SNA terminals. (What this means in terms of terminal features and processing independence is not altogether clear and warrants further definition.) Although most terminals contain some microprocessor logic that permits custom tailoring to user needs, this is not always the case. Table 6-1 ranks the intelligence and describes the capabilities of several SNA terminals.

SNA intelligence ranges from hard-wired and microprocessor-controlled devices at the low end to minicomputer controllers at the high end. IBM is moving more intelligent terminals and remote computing systems into its SNA offering; the company is also slowly providing users with flexible terminal devices and remote computing systems. For example, the 5280 Distributed Data System can be programmed in RPG and COBOL (mainframe compilation and central control) to perform extensive remote data editing and validation functions. Local data base query is not supported; implementing it would require a remote computing system. If local data base query is implemented using an 8100 Information System (operating under its Distributed Processing Program Executive [DPPX]), initiation of transactions between the 8100 and

Table 6-1. Intelligence Ranking

Category	Capabilities	IBM Terminal or Remote Computing System
Dumb	Terminal features and functions cannot be altered by users. Functions are specified only as preinstalled options.	3767 Communications Terminal 3630 Plant Communication System
Clever	Well-defined terminal functions can be altered by users after delivery by programming in the host or terminal.	3270 Information Display System 3600 Finance Communication System 3650 Retail Store System 3660 Supermarket System 5250 Information Display System 5520 Administrative System
Smart	Terminal operation can be altered by users through programming in a terminal-specific macro language; such operation is related to specified functions (e.g., data editing, media conversion).	3650 Communications System (programmable) 3680 Programmable Store System (POS) 3730 Distributed Office Communication System 3770 Data Communications System 3790 Communications System 6670 Information Distributor
Bright	Terminal operation can be tailored to user requirements by programming in a high-level language (e.g., RPG, COBOL, BASIC) or an assembler language, as required. Terminal-specific DBMS can support local data base query.	5280 Distributed Data System 8100 Information System System/34 System/38 Series/I 5120 Computing System

an IBM mainframe in an SNA network is not supported. IBM intends to provide such support in the future. IBM's movement toward providing intelligent and flexible terminals is undoubtedly slow and cautious. Other manufacturers, however, merely provide very powerful intelligent terminals. They still do not solve the problem of interfacing such terminals to the application programs in the mainframe in a way that will allow the programs to readily use the data processed on these terminals. The solution to that problem has been left to the user or to IBM.

SNA software will play the major role in the evolution of SNA. Initially, the software included only the network control program in the front-end processor and the telecommunications access method in the mainframe. The emphasis has shifted, however, from communications features to supporting the development of distributed processing application programs. SNA software has, therefore, grown to include transaction processing software, interactive support programs, remote job entry programs, mainframe programs supporting SNA remote-node software, and network design and management programs. SNA programs can be divided into four major categories:

- Operating system—This includes the actively supported mainframe operating systems; DOS/VSE, VS1, VM, and MVS; and their remote job entry subsystem components. These operating systems form the base on which the other SNA program products are assembled to construct the network.
- Application interface and support programs—These programs perform the end-user and presentation services functions in the mainframe. These functions ease application program development by isolating the

programmer from some of the details of formatting displays, controlling printer operations, and so on. The software includes transaction processing software (e.g., IMS/VS, CICS/VS), interactive support programs (e.g., TSO, VSPC), and mainframe programs supporting SNA remote-node software. This software must intimately interact with the terminal editing and formatting features. The greatest difficulty in interfacing non-SNA terminals to SNA networks lies in matching SNA features and commands to non-SNA display editing and formatting features.

- Telecommunications access methods—When IBM first introduced SNA, the virtual telecommunications access method (VTAM) was provided as the mainframe-resident access method and network manager. Today, VTAM, VTAME (for the 4300 processors), and TCAM are the principal access methods and network managers. These programs can be upgraded with MSNF to allow implementation of fully distributed IBM mainframe networks. The access methods allow application programs to share network resources and terminals (unlike pre-SNA methods, which required terminals to be dedicated to specific application programs). VTAM provides each application access to the network but requires the application to perform some telecommunications management functions (e.g., transmission scheduling, message queuing, error recovery). In contrast, TCAM manages the network, with little application program involvement. The TCAM message control program (MCP) performs telecommunications management functions for the application programs. Under TCAM, the session endpoint is the message queue, while VTAM's session endpoint is the application program. (Both TCAM and VTAM use buffers to smooth data flow between the terminals and the mainframe.) Despite these functional differences, the decision to use TCAM or VTAM/VTAME will be based primarily on which terminals, application interface programs, and high-level language interfaces are supported by IBM.

- Network control software—IBM offers its network control program/virtual storage (ACF/NCP/VS) only as the communications software resident in the 370x front-end communications controller. MSNF enhancements in the mainframe telecommunications access method work in conjunction with ACF/NCP/VS to provide dynamic sharing of network resources among a number of mainframe computers. ACF/NCP/VS is the primary mechanism for moving communications functions (e.g., line and buffer control, recoverable line-error handling, control-character insertion and deletion) out of the mainframe. ACF/NCP/VS can be extended to allow a 3705-II to support selected non-SNA terminals by addition of the network terminal option program, provided by IBM to aid in converting to SNA.

SNA software consists mainly of macroinstructions, which are translated into assembler language program modules. The macros are incorporated into other SNA programs or application processing programs written in such higher-level languages as COBOL. The central SNA programs created in this way are the telecommunications access method and the network control software. In order to define the network in these programs, it is necessary to know the physical configurations of both the mainframe with its local terminals and peripherals and the communications network with its devices. Such knowledge must encompass the terminal devices and how they will use the network resources (e.g., terminal-initiated network use versus application-program-initiated terminal use), the various communications lines (e.g., switched, nonswitched, satellite channels), and how the lines interconnect the terminals and the mainframe (e.g., point-to-point, multipoint, alternate routing). The system programmer must also be familiar with the mainframe's operating system, its use of telecommunications disk-resident libraries (e.g., for VTAM, TCAM, NCP), and how the access method views the application programs. The complexity of this procedure is indicative of SNA's overall complexity. A major criticism of SNA is that IBM, in an apparent effort to preserve its existing products, has created an abundance of overcomplex, inefficient products that do not provide all SNA design features. This situation should be mitigated as SNA continues to evolve; however, it may require 5 to 10 years to resolve the difficulties and make SNA less complex.

Application interface and support program enhancements (CICS/VS, IMS/VS) provide new SNA capabilities that allow programs and data bases to be spread over multiple IBM mainframes and to insulate the application programmer from this distribution. Although IBM's intent is to extend distribution to remote computing systems (e.g., the 8100 Information System), the supporting software products are still under development.

KEY SNA FEATURES

The key features of SNA include SDLC, the system services control point (SSCP), layering, network-addressable units (NAUs), and sessions. These features are discussed in the following paragraphs.

SDLC

The purpose of protocols is to open, manage, and close the data transmission process between network hardware components. SDLC, SNA's common communications protocol, is generally viewed as a single unifying protocol for SNA. In reality, it has several variations that differ in the commands and responses allowed between network hardware components. These essential differences allow SDLC to be used with different communications media (e.g., half-duplex point-to-point channels, multipoint full-duplex channels, looped channels).

SDLC differs from pre-SNA synchronous protocols because it is bit rather than character synchronous. SDLC commands are consequently a series of bit patterns that have no intrinsic meaning as members of a specific character set (e.g., ASCII or EBCDIC). The use of such commands makes SDLC more efficient by reducing transmission overhead. BSC commands, for example, require several 8-bit characters, while SDLC commands require a single 8-bit

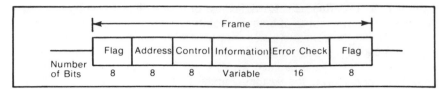

Figure 6-2. SDLC Frame

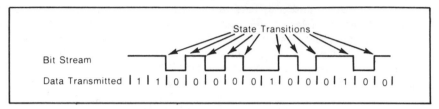

Figure 6-3. Invert-on-Zero Transmission Coding

field. Data transfer uses a single-frame format (see Figure 6-2). Synchronous identification of the sequential bits within each SDLC frame is ensured by the unique flags (a bit sequence of a zero, six ones, and a zero: 01111110) and invert-on-zero encoding of data transmitted in the frame (see Figure 6-3). The unique flag patterns ensure that a data stream will never contain all ones (and thus no state transitions in the bit stream), and synchronization between modem and terminal is maintained.

SDLC is transparent to the code structure of the data being transmitted over the network. Data transparency is ensured by the unique flag pattern and the information sequencing in the SDLC frame. Once an SDLC device begins transmission of a frame by sending a flag pattern, it monitors the bit stream for a sequence of five ones and inserts a zero after the fifth one. (The receiving device removes these zeros.) Because the flags are unique and occur only at the beginning and end of each frame, the receiving device can tell which information is in the address, command, error checking, and information fields by the position relative to the flag.

SDLC's most significant shortcoming is that it permits only seven frames to be unacknowledged by the receiver on a communications link. This is sufficient for most mainframe-to-terminal communications. When transmission occurs over satellite channels, however, with 300-millisecond one-way transmission delay and speeds of more than 9,600 bits per second, allowing only seven outstanding frames can severely reduce transmission efficiency and thereby increase transmission delays and response time.

SSCP

The system services control point (SSCP) is the SNA network manager for a single SNA domain. SSCP checks physical resources to ensure that they are active whenever their corresponding logical resources are active, coordinates communications between network elements, and retains error performance data. In complex multidomain SNA networks, each domain has its own SSCP, which communicates with the others, managing the network cooperatively. Because SSCP is resident in the access method in the mainframe, communications functions have not been distributed to any great degree, and SNA networks remain highly host dependent.

Layers

SNA groups related services into layers; each layer interacts with its adjacent layers in the SNA network. Originally, three major layers—the communications system layer, the transmission subsystem layer, and the common network layer—and several sublayers were identified. SNA layers have been further defined to include network-addressable unit services, function management data services, and data flow control layers within the communications system layer; transmission control within the transmission subsystem layer; and path control and data link control layers within the common network layer.

The layered approach is advantageous in allowing new features to be added by making changes in a single layer, without affecting hardware and software in other layers. (For example, MSNF was developed using changes to the path control layer and the SSCP.) In reality, of course, the SNA layers are conceptual entities, and their boundaries are not rigid. For example, parameters for function management data services and data flow control can be passed to the transmission control layer for inclusion in the request header that the latter appends to the data being transmitted. In addition, the telecommunications access-method software contains elements from the communications system layer and the transmission subsystem layer.

NAUs

Network-addressable units (NAUs) represent logical units, physical units, and SSCPs. Data transfers occur between these units, and each NAU has a unique network name and address assigned. The NAU separates the physical network elements from the logical network design of SNA, removing communications functions from application programs and isolating them in the hardware and software. The problem, however, is that NAUs must be defined several times when an SNA network is constructed: to the communications access method, the network control program, and frequently to the terminal controllers.

Sessions

Data transfer through an SNA network occurs in sessions (a session is a logical and physical path through the network connecting two NAUs, through which large amounts of data can be exchanged). Once a session is activated, its physical path is fixed. If deactivated and then reactivated, however, the new session might use a different path. If two application programs were to use the same terminal, two separate and distinct sessions would be required between

the terminal and each program, and the sessions could not be active simultaneously. An application program can have many sessions simultaneously active
with separate terminals under SNA. Session activation and deactivation are
controlled by the SSCP.

Sessions, however, present a problem in that they can be disrupted by
equipment malfunctions, requiring complete reestablishment before the teleprocessing can be completed. In contrast, a datagram approach—in which all
information required to control and route the information through the network
is in a self-contained packet—would make such malfunctions less disruptive.
(Most current architectures communicate by using sessions.)

SNA TODAY AND TOMORROW

The evolution of SNA has already allowed it to support increasingly complex networks; this trend is expected to continue well into this decade (see
Figure 6-4). First-generation SNA networks were simple, hierarchical,
mainframe-controlled communications networks; later multisystem networking facility enhancements supported distributed networks of IBM mainframes.
Current SNA networks can support interconnection of remote computing
systems to these networks, using multiple communications channels with
alternate routing. The evolution of SNA has mainly provided the software
tools that support communications in these complex networks. Emphasis is
now shifting toward providing tools to assist programmers in developing
distributed processing and data base systems while insulating them from the
problems of coordinating operations among several computer systems. IBM is
now identifying application-to-application services as part of the network-
addressable unit services layer, the highest described in current SNA product
literature. These services allow application programs to communicate without
concern for the details of the network; in some cases, an application program
will be allowed to access a data base without knowing its location in the
network. Such capabilities are provided through enhancements to SNA's application interface and support programs (e.g., CICS/VS, IMS/VS).

Network Operations Management

Network operations management has also evolved significantly. Current
SNA software products assist in managing complex SNA networks, helping to:
- Control daily operations
- Identify data transmission problems
- Measure and report network performance
- Track the resolution of network problems
- Coordinate implementation of network changes

These products must be viewed as the first step toward centralized network
operations control. Much remains to be done, particularly in the area of
identifying and isolating data transmission problems, before true network
operations management is achieved.

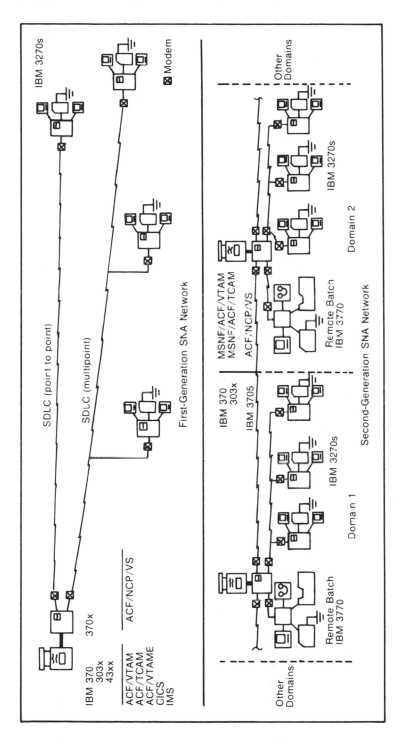

Figure 6-4. SNA Network Evolution

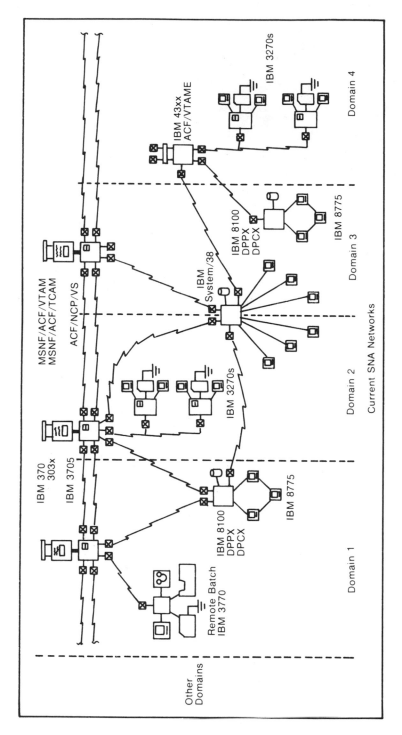

Figure 6-4. (cont)

Reference Model

The International Standards Organization proposed its Open Systems Inter-connection reference model for a telecommunications system architecture, with the goal of making such systems compatible. Because of its architectural similarity to this model, SNA can be adapted to conform to the proposed standards (see Figure 6-5). The lower levels of the OSI architecture, for example, map directly into SNA, and SDLC is a subset of the OSI link-control-level HDLC protocol. Conforming to the architectural model will not necessarily eliminate the difficulty of telecommunications system compatibility. Interfaces with adjacent and/or equivalent levels must be explicitly and clearly defined to ensure true compatibility. A considerable amount of work must be completed to define the interfaces in both hardware and software.

CCITT X.25

The CCITT X.25 recommendation for the interface to packet-switched networks implements the first three levels of the OSI model. Although X.25 and SNA have similar features (both can use the V.24 interface for the physical control layer and a bit-synchronous protocol for the link control layer), direct

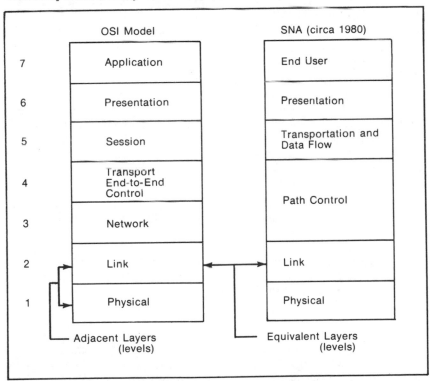

Figure 6-5. ISO OSI/SNA Comparison

compatibility does not exist. The incompatibilities arise in part because X.25 is a 3-layer interface between data terminal equipment (DTE) and a packet network, while SNA ensures information exchange in six architectural layers between two ends of a network (e.g., two DTEs or an application program and a terminal). IBM does provide (as a separate unit) an X.25-to-SNA interface that maps SNA links into X.25 virtual circuits at the network layer (Layer 3) and uses a link access procedure (LAP) variation of the HDLC protocol for the link control layer (Layer 2). The V.24 interface is used for the physical layer (Layer 1). As both X.25 and SNA mature, this interface will change as well, with the link access procedure balanced (LAPB) and the X.21 physical interface likely to be used in Layers 2 and 1, respectively.

CONCLUSION

IBM's SNA represents the comprehensive and cohesive approach of the world's largest mainframe manufacturer to the design and implementation of teleprocessing and distributed DP networks. SNA supports the construction of large and expensive networks; the cost of implementation (with its increased resource requirements) keeps many of SNA's technically advanced features beyond the reach of small- and medium-sized DP installations. Regardless of installation size, however, SNA will still provide some benefits. For example, data transmission using SDLC is more efficient than it is using BSC. In addition, IBM's commitment to the continuing evolution of SNA will cause many users to add SNA products selectively to their IBM-mainframe-based networks; few will totally embrace SNA.

SNA's translation from design to hardware and software products is still incomplete and in many cases leaves much to be desired in performance and simplicity. Although many SNA products complexities may be unwarranted, IBM has the ability and apparently the desire to correct these design and implementation deficiencies. As SNA matures and continues to evolve, its current problems will likely be replaced by new problems. With any problem, old or new, users have a choice: to correct the problem through modifications to IBM equipment (or other means) or to await a solution from IBM.

Several management strategies, such as the following, can be pursued when upgrading an existing system or building and implementing a new distributed system.

Strategy 1. This strategy involves using all IBM SNA components for the system and AT&T channels for communications. This is a good strategy for a new application and system; however, for upgrading an existing system, whether IBM or non-IBM based, it can be expensive.

Strategy 2. In this strategy, the IBM SNA components would be selectively replaced with equivalent components offered by independent manufacturers, thus providing increased performance, reduced cost, and greater reliability. IBM components would be retained only if no suitable replacements could be found. This is a difficult strategy for implementing a new system and upgrading a non-IBM-based system; it is a good strategy for users upgrading an existing IBM-based system.

Strategy 3. No IBM equipment is used in this strategy; implementation uses a minicomputer manufacturer's architecture. This is a good strategy for a new system and for a non-IBM system upgrade; it is possible to use it for upgrading an IBM-based system.

Strategy 4. This involves doing nothing but waiting. As a strategy for a new application and system, it is bad; it is, however, a possible strategy for upgrading both IBM- and non-IBM-based systems.

Depending upon the user and the environment, one of these strategies may prove best in terms of cost, performance, ease of use, and reliability.

7 SNA-like Architectures and Capabilities

by Joseph St. Amand

INTRODUCTION

IBM's 1974 introduction of System Network Architecture (SNA) represented, among other things, the company's entry into the field of data communications (as opposed to data processing). SNA provides its users with significant capabilities unattainable with earlier IBM hardware and software. Although impressed by these capabilities, some network managers are attempting to attain SNA's enhancements and to avoid some of the less-than-desirable features of current implementations. Although significant improvements in implementation have been made since 1974, much remains to be done. Critics of SNA, while acknowledging its clear superiority over earlier IBM offerings, call attention to its failings:

- Expense—Implementing SNA is expensive because it requires the most recent (and costly) hardware and software released by IBM.
- Complexity—This is caused, in part, by the involvement of host software (the access method) in controlling communications. SNA complexity also affects personnel training adversely in terms of time and expense.
- Lack of flexibility—This is evident in the procedures required to make such network changes as adding trunks or nodes and adding or removing terminals.
- Lack of an X.25 interface—Because of the SNA premise that data is transferred over leased or switched lines secured from a common carrier, no provision was made for an X.25 interface to a public data network.
- Incompatibility with non-IBM products—Compatibility with other vendors' products was not an SNA design consideration.
- Lack of efficient network control—Network control is allocated to dedicated hosts with special software, a strategy that is both expensive and risky.

Some vendors of IBM plug-compatible communications processors provide extremely good replacements for their IBM counterparts. Communications software that resides in the communications processor shifts the focus of network control from the host to the communications processor. Thus, some data communications equipment firms can provide SNA capability, remove deficiencies associated with the IBM implementation, and enable capabilities not found in SNA.

SNA CAPABILITIES

SNA provides a number of significant and desirable functional capabilities:
- An operator at a given terminal can access all application programs resident in any host defined in the network.
- The network can be monitored and controlled from centralized locations with some independence from the application hosts.
- Remote modem diagnostics can be performed.
- Dynamic and transparent rerouting (alternate routing) is possible in the event of line failure.
- Different classes of service are available.
- Devices can be added and removed without system regeneration (dynamic reconfiguration).

Full SNA implementation requires the following hardware and software products (discussed in a later section of this chapter):
- A host-resident access method (ACF/TCAM/MSNF or ACF/VTAM/ MSNF)
- The 3705-II communications processor
- The synchronous data link control protocol (SDLC)
- Special communications processor software (ACF/NCP/VS)
- A dedicated host for network control
- Special software for network monitoring and control (NPDA, NCCF)
- Special SNA terminals
- New microprocessor-based diagnostic modems

Host control of communications is central to the architecture of SNA: a system service control point (SSCP) controls a domain of resources, including communications processors.

Other Vendor Products

Other vendors provide the capabilities of SNA with different strategies and products. Some manufacture hardware that is plug compatible with IBM SNA devices. Others, such as Digital Equipment Corporation, provide SNA protocol emulators that permit their systems to participate in IBM/SNA networks. Still other vendors provide true alternatives to SNA (based on alternative architectures) for a network with IBM hosts and terminals.

Both NCR-Comten and Computer Communications Inc (CCI) specialize in manufacturing communications processors (the 3690 and CC-85, respectively) that are plug compatible with IBM and, in an IBM network, that can replace the IBM 3705-II communications processor. Both the 3690 and CC-85 support such peripherals as magnetic tape units, card readers, line printers, and consoles; and Comten or CCI software modules replace the IBM front-end software (ACF/NCP/VS).

It should be understood that this discussion of CCI and Comten products is not an endorsement. The products are used as illustrations because of their demonstrated ability to support otherwise-IBM networks with architecture that is as extensive as SNA and to point out that such alternatives do exist. Both CCI and NCR-Comten have fully developed communications architectures in which control of communications resides in communications processors rather than in the hosts. Both vendors provide a communications network linking IBM hosts, terminals, and peripherals.

Most recent SNA releases allow for cross-domain data communications between elements of a distributed network that is composed of numerous hosts and thousands of terminals. NCR-Comten and CCI architectures also provide this capability (see Figure 7-1). The architectures are implemented through families of IBM plug-compatible communications processors and proprietary software (discussed in the following sections).

HARDWARE

Either the IBM 3705-I or 3705-II communications controller must be present in each domain of an SNA network. Certain network configurations and capabilities, however, require hardware options available only with the 3705-II

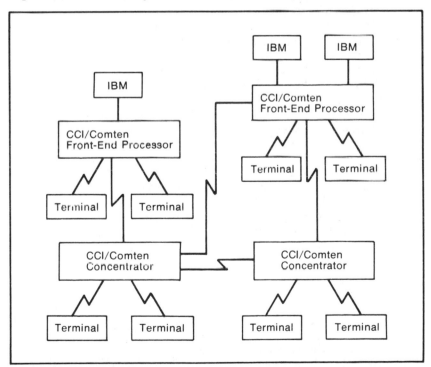

Figure 7-1. CCI/Comten Control of Communications in a Multidomain Network

communications controller (IBM's most powerful controller to date, which is similar to Comten's 3690 and CCI's CC-85). The 3690, Comten's newest communications processor, provides greater speed and capabilities than its predecessors as well as a wide range of possible applications and environments.

CCI's CC-85 is a high-throughput communications front end that can be used with the IBM 260/370, 303x, and compatible mainframes. The company's most powerful processor, it succeeds the older CC-80 and offers a sustained 400K-byte-per-second capacity as a functional replacement for the 3705; peak throughput approaches 1M byte per second. The CC-85 can also be used as a message switcher, a remote concentrator, a standalone communications processor, or a combination of these functions.

Both the 3690 and the CC-85 offer higher throughput, more line connections (512 and 1,232, respectively), and more flexible software than the 3705-II; they also support a larger number of hosts.

SOFTWARE

IBM Software

SNA Telecommunications Access Methods. The communications access method is the key to SNA and is a major component of the host operating system. This method handles the interaction between the host application programs and the local communications controller. Within an SNA system, either the Telecommunications Access Method (TCAM) or Virtual Telecommunications Access Method (VTAM) is required. TCAM is a queued access method designed to handle messages arriving at an unpredictable rate; it was IBM's first SNA communications access method. Best suited to the IBM user migrating toward SNA, TCAM can support a wide variety of mixed BSC, asynchronous, and SDLC devices. VTAM, on the other hand, provides immediate access to host application programs and best serves the user whose network consists predominantly of SNA/SDLC devices.

ACF/TCAM and ACF/VTAM. Introduced by IBM in 1976, the Advanced Communications Function (ACF), with separate program product enhancements for both TCAM and VTAM, enables the interconnection of different operating systems and hosts, whether in the same or separate locations. An additional program enhancement, the Multisystem Networking Facility (MSNF), was required for each access method involved in an interconnected network.

Multisystem Networking. The multisystem capability allows any supported terminal in the network full access to any application program in any connected host. The access method, in conjunction with the communications processor (loaded with a similar ACF program), provides network transparency to both the application and the terminal. The terminal operator need not even know which host controls the application being used. Without MSNF, terminal and line switching from one host system to another could be achieved only through host-system operator commands or user-programmed procedures.

A systems services control point (SSCP) is part of the access method driving an SNA network. The SSCP is actually the switchboard logic for the system; it contains a matrix of defined communications parameters for each addressable element in the network.

All network elements defined to the SSCP comprise the system's domain. An addressable unit may belong to only one domain, even if more than one access method is resident in the same host (as in MVS or VM/370 configurations). MSNF, however, enables cross-domain communications. It provides the access method with the capability to locate a foreign resource, obtain the necessary information for session establishment, and initiate a session between the element of its domain and the foreign resource.

Advanced Communications Function for Network Control Program/ Virtual Storage (ACF/NCP/VS). This software module is resident in the 3705-II and manages the details of line control and the routing of data through the network. The access method sends control parameters to the NCP, directing it to perform specific operations. The NCP in turn controls the network operation and provides the access method with its required data and the resulting status information. The access method directs the network channel speeds; the NCP and the communications controller are responsible for line control and data transfer.

Network Communications Control Facility (NCCF). The NCCF is used to monitor and control an SNA network. (A more detailed description is provided in the Network Control section.)

Network Problem Determination Application (NPDA). NPDA assists users in performing communications network problem determination, collecting records of detected errors. (NPDA is described more fully in the Network Control section.)

CCI Software

CCI's network communications system (NCS) for the CC-85 consists of two key modules, the NCS-1.4 and the NCS-4. The NCS message-switching capabilities can be custom tailored to user requirements, and a comprehensive store-and-forward message-switching network can be implemented.

NCS-1.4. Advanced versions of this module provide line handling, independent of host control. Less sophisticated versions (in emulation mode) offer line-handling functions, such as polling and error handling, under host control. This module provides the network operator with commands for monitoring and modifying the network. A CRT control console allows retrieval of error conditions, line and host statistics, and so on.

NCS-4. This module provides the networking capability for the CC-85. Its intercomputer communications protocol controls data interchange between network nodes. The protocol also provides selective retransmission, a feature that permits retransmission of only a packet received in error rather than the erroneous frame and all subsequent packets (as is required in other network schemes).

Electronic Mail System. The recently released electronic mail system (EMS), an enhancement of the message-switching system, adds public and private electronic mailbox services to CCI's message-switching services.

EMS supports local and remote terminals and computers using dial-in and dial-out or dedicated line facilities, with synchronous or asynchronous protocols. It can be used for interactive or batch message entry, allowing users to edit messages; send them; obtain a summary of messages in a mailbox; and read, answer, reroute, and purge messages. Electronic billboard services (public mailboxes) allow common messages to be shared by a group of users. Both short- and long-term message retention are provided; short-term messages are automatically purged after a predetermined period. It should be noted that these capabilities are not available with existing implementations of SNA.

NCR-Comten Software

Software for the 3690 is available in five major modules that provide network control, emulation, data switching, a communications networking system, and an interface to an X.25 packet network.

Comten-NCP. The network control program (NCP) is similar to IBM's NCP and, in one version, allows the 3690 to emulate a 3705-II that is running a similar version (ACF/NCP/VS). New versions of NCP are usually available from Comten shortly after similar IBM releases.

Emulation. Emulation, which allows a 3690 to perform the same function(s) as the IBM device(s) it replaces, is performed by hardware rather than software, providing considerable network configuration flexibility. The program handles path completion from terminal line to host subchannel address and remains transparent to the host.

CNS. The communications networking system (CNS) supports dedicated and switched lines, multiple line speeds, and asynchronous, BSC, and SDLC terminals. Using this module, data is transferred between geographically separate 3690s over a full-duplex high-speed trunk.

DSS. The data-switching system (DSS) allows a 3690 to perform like a host node in the SNA environment, controlling SNA resources, or like a nodal processor in an SNA distributed-processor network. SNA/SDLC capabilities (similar to those for the 3705-II under ACF/NCP) are supported. Because DSS can co-reside with NCP and CNS, NCP capabilities are enhanced in the areas of message switching, basic message handling and queuing, and network security and control.

X.25-1. A system of software modules for 36xx communications processors, these modules provide an interface to an X.25 packet-switching network, support for virtual connections, effective utilization of the network's capabilities, and front-end processor functions for its virtual circuits.

SNA Functionality without SNA

From the user's perspective, one of the most glaring defects of IBM's pre-SNA architecture is the need to dedicate a terminal to one application per communications link. Control units are attached to a single communications line, which is assigned a host subchannel address. Each subchannel address in turn is assigned to one host application program. Consequently, all terminals on a given communications line are limited to one application program in one specific host processor; 3270 devices, communications lines, and control units are therefore dedicated to unique applications. Both CCI and NCR-Comten avoid this rigidity by permitting access to multiple applications with pre-SNA software. In neither case are modifications made to host software (operating system, access method, application).

Dynamic-application switching (DAS), an optional feature of CCI's NCS-1.4, allows the switching of certain start-stop devices (TTY and IBM 2741-type terminals) from one application to another in the same or a different host. The user can select from 16 applications residing in as many as six hosts. DAS lines can be leased, dial-up, or auto-baud rate detect; polled lines are not supported.

Multipoint dynamic application switching (MDAS) allows switching certain BSC devices (3270-type terminals) from one application to a different one in the same or another host. As with DAS, 16 host applications can reside on as many as six hosts.

NCR-Comten provides similar capability for the IBM 3270-type devices. The multiple-access facility (MAF) option available with the emulation module allows the device to select any application on any host defined in the network. MAF also reduces nonproductive polling by the host by placing the polling functions in the communications processor.

By allowing data exchange between dispersed nodes controlled by different hosts, NCS-4 and CNS provide multisystem networking capabilities similar to IBM's MSNF in SNA, without requiring a change to ACF/TCAM or ACF/VTAM.

PUBLIC DATA NETWORKS

The use of a public data network (PDN) can be an effective means of reducing costs and improving service. Volume-sensitive PDNs provide alternatives to distance-sensitive leased or dial-up lines. Within the continental United States, access is available to three such carriers: GTE-Telenet, Tymnet, and Uninet. The concern with PDNs in this chapter lies in:

- The extent of the added value
- The ability of a vendor to provide a PDN interface

- The ability of a PDN to provide an interface for IBM hosts and terminals

Added Value

In some respects, PDNs are themselves alternatives to SNA, providing
such services as:
- Access to multiple hosts and applications from a given terminal
- Network control
- Alternate routing in the event of failure
- Nondisruptive reconfiguration
- Routing data along the most efficient path
- Converting data from one character set to another
- Adjusting transmission speed for maximum data flow while maintain-
  ing data integrity
- Reducing the probability of undetected errors (Tymnet claims 1 in 4 $\times$
  10^{10} bits)

Tymnet also provides a store-and-forward electronic mail service (On
Tyme) that can be accessed from terminals used for other applications.

Access To PDNs

At the present time, NCR-Comten and IBM are certified for limited access
to GTE-Telenet, and CCI is being tested for certification by GTE-Telenet and
Tymnet.

NCR-Comten's X.25 Interface Revision 1 includes packet adapters, net-
work call-processing software, and X.25 interfaces for DATAPAC and GTE-
Telenet. The packet adapters allow start-stop terminals attached to an X.25
PDN to appear as emulation program start-stop terminals. Release 2 of the
X.25 interface will include capabilities of Revision 1, statistics collection, and
support for:
- NCP start-stop terminals
- SNA terminals
- NCP/MAF BSC 3270 terminals
- CNS trunk links through X.25 virtual circuits
- 36xx remote communications processor interfaces to X.25 PDNs

In May 1981, GTE-Telenet certified an IBM X.25 interface for Series/1
minicomputers. This is not, however, the long-awaited gateway to SNA
networks. The present arrangement permits a Series/1 minicomputer to exchange data with a second Series/1 using GTE-Telenet as the carrier. The
message-switching and routing functions needed to interface with an SNA
network on the other side are not provided, however, nor is an X.25 interface
for the end user.

IBM offers this limited X.25 interface on a programming request price
quotation (PRPQ) basis. This is consistent with IBM's decision to sell the
Series/1 as a quasi-OEM product. Similar X.25 support is planned for the 5280
intelligent workstation and for the 8100 distributed processing system.

3270 Support

Two of the U.S.-based PDNs provide linking of IBM 3270s to packet-switched networks:

- TYMNET uses node-resident software to support 3270s attached to a cluster controller (linked to the TYMNET node) and a multidrop leased line between the node and user terminals. No changes are made to host or front-end processor software.
- GTE-Telenet also makes provisions for connecting 3270s, placing a Telenet processor at the user site. A special software package is used for the IBM host/X.25 interface (DMEP) in the IBM 370x front-end processor. Unlike TYMNET, GTE-Telenet does not support multidrop leased lines; terminals must be connected by means of cluster controllers. GTE-Telenet provides SNA functionality—access to multiple programs in multiple hosts—without requiring SNA products (using DMEP and TP protocol converters, products of Cambridge Telecommunications).
- Uninet does not support the IBM 3270 or any other synchronous terminal; support is restricted to ASCII or IBM 2741-type terminals.

NETWORK CONTROL

The primary purpose of network control is to minimize downtime. Successful network control therefore monitors the network to identify probable sources of failure before the fact, quickly reallocates available resources after the fact, and provides prompt isolation and correction of the failure.

IBM

IBM has divided multiprocessor network control between host-resident and communications-processor-resident software. Two host-resident programs (NCCF and NPDA) control and monitor the SNA network. The network communications control facility (NCCF) provides a program base for communications network management. The network problem determination application (NPDA), which is used with NCCF, assists in the diagnosis of network problems in a multidomain network. An NCCF (prerequisite for NPDA) must reside in each domain to achieve systemwide network control.

Release 3 of ACF/NCP has enhanced communications-processor-based control of the network, with significantly improved connectivity, flow control, routing, availability, and network management. NCCF and NPDA, loaded in a system/370, 303x, or 4300, allow commands and messages to be submitted and received through display consoles. IBM's network control capacity has been significantly enhanced by the use of tapes, disks, and remote operator stations.

It is estimated that the minimum storage required for NCCF with a single operator is 365K bytes; the actual amount, of course, depends on both NCCF definitions and the network size and configuration. NPDA adds 160K bytes to the NCCF virtual storage requirement (direct-access requirements depend on network size). NCCF and NPDA do not, however, require a dedicated network-control processor.

NCR-Comten

Peripherals (e.g., card readers, line printers, disks, and network consoles) can be attached to Comten's communications processors (this is not possible with the IBM processors). A network control center can be established within the 3690, and a message control program module containing a network manager is available. The network manager provides a centralized control function for multiple-node networks; it handles the command, control, monitoring, and reporting functions. The manager also aids in network implementation, maintenance, modification, and operation. A separate maintenance processing program helps isolate problems.

Computer activity can be measured and recorded by such performance products as Dynaprobe, which monitors events in the central processor, operating system, peripherals, and applications. The performance data is software converted and formatted into reports that can be visually analyzed.

CCI

A CRT console directly connected to the central processing unit controls the CC-85. The console and software perform monitoring and tracing functions and provide users with considerable control over the network teleprocessing activities. An NCS-1.4 monitor allows network event and condition reports to be displayed as they occur. More than 60 error and event conditions are recognized, reported, displayed in color, and recorded in mass storage.

Statistical Information

IBM, CCI, and NCR-Comten all recognize the importance of accumulating statistics as a means of anticipating failures and increasing resource-utilization efficiency. All three provide collection, organization, and display of error statistics as well as data about communications controllers, lines, modems, cluster controllers, control units, and terminals. They also provide storage of error and status information for later retrieval.

Although all three vendors provide the means to control a large multiple-host network, the IBM approach differs considerably from those of the others. SNA requires a dedicated station (host or console) with special software for each domain of a multidomain network, while CCI and NCR-Comten integrate network control into standard communications processor software.

FUTURE POSSIBILITIES

It is likely that standard off-the-shelf X.25 interfaces to PDNs will be available in the near future and will be suitable for a wide variety of terminals and hosts from IBM, CCI, and NCR-Comten. IBM and CCI will introduce new communications processors, and new software from CCI will be able to support SNA/SDLC devices.

Providing a standard off-the-shelf X.25 interface to a PDN is possibly the top issue in data communications at this time. IBM is under intense pressure to provide the capability that would permit any SNA device to communicate with any other SNA device over a PDN with the flexibility of an all-SNA network. (The Series/1-to-Series/1 capability described previously leaves much to be desired.) It is anticipated that IBM will provide a genuine X.25 gateway to an SNA network in the near future. NCR-Comten's X.25 Interface Revision 2, when available, will provide genuine PDN support for the vast majority of terminal types currently in use, and CCI is expected to announce an approved X.25 interface shortly.

Although CCI cannot, at present, support IBM's SNA products, the company has indicated that a new series of communications processors and software is forthcoming that may alter that situation. This added capability may eventually cause CCI's architectural structure to be renamed distributed network architecture (DNA). The DNA line will probably support IBM SNA terminals and allow interconnection between a DNA communications processor and a 3705.

The 3705 has, of course, been available since 1973. It is eclipsed in performance by both the 3690 and the CC-85, and it is possible that its successor will be announced soon. While emulation mode support may not be available, some X.25 capabilities might be included as standard options. Standalone capability may also be enhanced, supporting such peripherals as mass disk storage.

CONCLUSION

Data communications has supplanted DP as the area most likely to yield increased efficiency and reduced costs in the coming decade. Established DP centers with several applications and extensive data communications can conceivably benefit from the network capabilities described in this chapter. Telecommunications managers who wish to capitalize on recent and ongoing improvements in data communications might find the following suggestions helpful:

- Existing networks should be examined for inefficiencies and/or unsatisfactory performance resulting from limitations in pre-SNA hardware and software.

- The ways in which SNA can improve data communications should be considered.
- The potential for increased functionality, flexibility, and cost reduction offered by other vendors (e.g., CCI, NCR-Comten, GTE-Telenet, Tymnet) should be considered.
- A cost/benefit analysis of alternative implementations should be performed.

The two common examples of earlier IBM network inefficiencies—the dedication of terminals and data links to a specific application in a specific host and the dedication of data links to specific terminal types (speed, data link control)—can be circumvented by both CCI and NCR-Comten, without requiring transition to SNA.

When vendors are given a clear statement of a data communications problem, they generally propose solutions—at no cost to the user. Armed with the knowledge that alternative means exist for attaining the enhancements provided by SNA, the network manager should thoroughly investigate all possibilities in seeking the implementation that best satisfies his or her unique requirements.

⑧ Encryption for Data Security

by Dr. Rein Turn

INTRODUCTION

An important responsibility of communications managers is maintaining control over the use of corporate data communications systems and their data. To achieve this, it is necessary to use a variety of safeguards. A major goal is to prevent occurrences of computer crime—employee use of corporate DP systems for the perpetration of white-collar crimes or the penetration of the system by outsiders [1]. Computer systems have been used, for example, to maintain fictitious employees on payroll, order fictitious deliveries of products, and manipulate corporate assets and finances [2].

The problem of detecting computer-aided crime is compounded by the nature of information processing, storage, and transmission in computer systems. For example:
- Data is usually stored in media not directly readable by people.
- Data can be erased or modified without leaving evidence.
- Computerized records do not have seals or signatures to verify authenticity or distinguish copies from originals.
- Data can be accessed and manipulated from remote terminals.
- Transactions are performed at high speeds without human monitoring or control.
- Programs specifying the processing rules are stored in the same media as data and therefore can also be easily manipulated.

Although these examples also represent some of the reasons for using computers in the first place, they make management control difficult.

In addition to controlling use of the computer system by authorized employees, the problems associated with employees who may have access to the computer but are not authorized to use programs or access data files and the problems with individuals who are outside the organization should be considered. Such people may attempt to bypass system safeguards in order to browse in files, capture control of the operating system [3], or eavesdrop on communications links. Eavesdropping is relatively simple for anyone with some technical skill and resources, even in microwave transmission links [4]. The emergence of low-cost portable intelligent terminals makes sophisticated wiretapping possible: a terminal can be inserted into the communications link to intercept, modify, and retransmit data. Experiments have proved such piggyback penetration of computer systems feasible [5].

Another problem has been the absence of signatures or other authenticating material in digital messages. When two parties enter into a legally binding relationship by exchanging digital messages, each should require assurance that the messages are authentic and cannot be altered.

Whether a given system is a probable target for internal or external computer crime depends on several factors:
- The nature of the organization and its operations
- Types of applications and data bases in the DP system
- Opportunities for economic gain for the perpetrators
- The size of the system's user population
- The type of system and the capabilities available to users

For example, a remote time-shared system that allows users to submit assembly language programs offers more opportunities for computer crime than does a system limiting its users to a fixed set of predefined transactions.

The potential threats against a DP system and the losses that may result are sufficient reason for security risk assessment [6, 7]; unfortunately, effective methodologies and techniques have not yet been developed [8]. It is important, therefore, to incorporate security safeguards during the system design phase rather than add them later. System designers must recognize that security measures have become as important in design criteria as other functional capabilities.

The trend toward distributed computer systems with remote terminals, processors, and data bases and the use of such systems for transmitting electronic mail accentuate the need for message authentication and secure data communications links. The use of cryptographic techniques for these purposes and the implications for the data communications manager are topics of this chapter.

BASIC METHODS

Protecting sensitive information in a communications channel (outside the physical control of the communicators) is essential [9]. Basically, there are two methods for providing protection:
1. Concealing the existence of the message by such techniques as including it with unrelated communications
2. Making the information in the message unintelligible through cryptographic techniques, without attempting to conceal the existence of the message

The latter approach is the more practical in computer/communications systems.

As illustrated in Figure 8-1, a cryptographic system (cryptosystem) for secure communications between a sender (S) and a receiver (R) consists of the following elements:

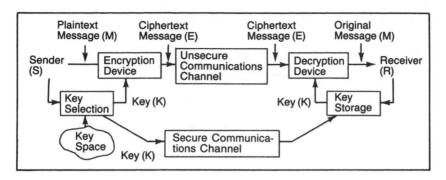

Figure 8-1. Application of Cryptographic Transformations

- A plaintext message (M) to be transmitted and protected
- A very large family of invertible cryptographic transformations (ciphers) (T) applied to M to produce ciphertext (E) and later to recover M by applying the inverse T^{-1} to E.
- A parameter (K, the key of the cryptosystem) that selects one specific transformation (T_K) from the family of transformations

A cryptosystem can be effective only if the communicators keep the key secret and the family T is large enough that the correct K could not be guessed or determined by trial-and-error search techniques.

Such a system is used in the following manner. Prior to proceeding with communication, both S and R agree upon the family of transformations to be used and establish K (e.g., one communicator selects K and communicates it to the other over a secure communications channel). Now S generates M and encrypts it by applying T_K: $E = T_K$ (M). The sender then transmits E. Upon receiving E, R applies the inverse transformation and recovers M: $M = T_K^{-1}$ (E). E may be intercepted in the channel and subjected to various cryptanalytic attacks aimed at M, K, or both. Since it must be assumed that the interceptor knows in detail the transformation being used, the security of the message rests entirely upon the interceptor not knowing which key was used.

More than 70 years ago, a set of effectiveness criteria for cryptosystems was stated by Kerkhoffs (as described by Shannon [10]):
- The transformation used should be unbreakable (if not in theory, then in practice).
- The interceptor's knowledge of the family of transformations being used and of the cryptosystem equipment should not compromise the protection provided.
- The key should be capable of providing all protection and should be easy to generate, store, transmit, and change.
- The transformation used should be simple, requiring no complicated rules or mental strain.

Although Kerkhoff's criteria were derived for manually operated communications systems, they can be applied to computer/communications systems.

Some changes, of course, have occurred. For example, computers permit more complex transformations, and the keys can be changed more readily and frequently. On the other hand, computers have become important tools for cryptanalysis, and their use has greatly reduced the effectiveness of classical cryptographic transformations [11].

In classical cryptography, all transformations are substitutions, transpositions, or product ciphers (combinations of substitutions and transpositions). If M is regarded as a string of characters from an alphabet (A), such as the English alphabet, a monoalphabetic substitution transformation replaces every character of A by either a character from a cipher alphabet (B) or a group of characters from B. These two cases are called monographic and polygraphic substitutions. Alphabet B is usually a permutation of A. A very simple form of a monoalphabetic substitution is the Caesar cipher, in which the cipher B is obtained by rotating the original alphabet A by a fixed number of character positions. This number is the key. Figure 8-2 illustrates a Caesar cipher in which K = 3 and A is rotated to the left. Because there are only 25 possible rotations for the English alphabet, this system is very easy to solve by trial-and-error methods.

Plaintext
alphabet A: a b c d e f g h i j k l m n o p q r s t u v w x y z

Ciphertext
alphabet B: d e f g h i j k l m n o p q r s t u v w x y z a b c

Plaintext message: sell all shares
Ciphertext: vhoo doo vkduhv

Figure 8-2. Caesar Cipher (K = 3)

Polyalphabetic substitution transformations use several cipher alphabets (B_1, B_2, . . . , B_n), each of which is usually a Caesar cipher. They are used cyclically to determine which substitution is to be made. The key can be numeric (showing the amount of rotation for each alphabet used) or alphabetic (showing which character of each of the alphabets corresponds to the plaintext letter "a"). For example, when the key is "domino," the plaintext message "sell all shares" is encrypted as "vsxt nzo gtiesy." The longer the key (the more alphabets used), the more effective a polyalphabetic substitution is because it hides the original text more thoroughly. If K is at least as long as the message, the key is generated by a random process and is used only once. This cryptosystem is called a Vernam system and is, in theory and practice, unbreakable. Its use in data communications systems, however, is impractical because a very large K must be provided when the message volume is large.

Transpositions are rearrangements of characters in a message, without changing the alphabet. Typically, a transposition operation is applied to a block of characters of the message. The key specifies which characters are to be interchanged. For example, in a block of six characters, with K specified as (136542), the word "profit" is changed to "optrfi." Character 3 replaces character 1, 6 replaces 3, and so forth as specified by the key until, finally, character 2 replaces 1. If the block is large, a transposition can be very effective.

Product transformations (repeated application of substitutions and transpositions) can be very effective "mixing transformations." One such transformation is the Data Encryption Standard (DES), approved by the National Bureau of Standards for nonmilitary agencies of the federal government [12]. DES is discussed in more detail in the next section. Other transformations, based on complex mathematical formulas [13], are also examined.

Transformations based on substitutions only are called stream ciphers—each character of the message is encrypted independently of the others and can be transmitted as soon as it has been encrypted. Transformations that apply transpositions are called block ciphers because an entire block of characters must be encrypted before any can be transmitted. The following types are based on the structure of the communication and the implementation of encryption:

- End-to-end encryption—The sender encrypts the message and it remains encrypted while being transmitted through a network until it is received and decrypted by the recipient.
- Link-by-link encryption—Each communications link from switching center to switching center has its own encryption key. The communicators need only the key to the nearest switching center.
- Super encryption—The communications system uses link-by-link encryption, but the communicators use their own end-to-end encryption keys.

Link-by-link encryption increases key security by limiting each communicator to only one key to the nearest switching center and eliminating the need to make prior key transmissions. This means, however, that communicators are placing their trust in the communications system and its security. Messages must be decrypted at each switching center for reencryption for the next link and can thus be intercepted at the switching centers. Super encryption can avoid this problem.

THE DATA ENCRYPTION STANDARD (DES)

In 1977, the National Bureau of Standards approved DES as a federal standard. The bureau decreed DES the only transformation to be used by civilian domestic agencies of the federal government [12]. DES has been published in full detail; its effectiveness derives from its complexity, the number of possible keys (more than 10^{16}), and the security of the keys used. DES is very resistant to cryptanalytic attacks, even by a large-scale use of computers, although its absolute security has been questioned [14]. It has been claimed that one million special-purpose microprocessors (given the plaintext message and corresponding ciphertext, each microprocessor searching for the correct key at a rate of one million per second) could conceivably find the key within one day. The possibility of such a facility is not likely, however, in the near future.

Because of DES's use in both government and private-sector communications systems, it is described here in some detail. The DES transformation is an iterative nonlinear block product cipher that operates on 64-bit data blocks. It is very complex and suitable only for application by computer. Special-purpose integrated-circuit chips have been developed for DES and are commercially available (see reference 15). The DES algorithm is used in reverse for decrypting the ciphertext (using the same key, of course). The key is also a 64-bit word, of which 8 are parity bits; thus, the effective key length is 56 bits.

None of the operations is secret—the permutations used, the method of selecting key bits, and the method of expanding to a 48-bit length are published in full detail [12]. The protection accorded M derives from the complexity of the transformation and the number of possible keys. Since the theory of the operation of DES is not available, there are no guidelines for modifying DES that, for example, permit encrypting a larger block of data at a time or using fewer iterations while still having an effective transformation. Clearly, programming DES operations in software would result in very slow operation of the encryption device and, consequently, the communications channel. In microcircuit versions of DES, however, device data rates of up to 1.6 megabits per second can be supported. The cost of a DES device ranges from $1,000 to $5,000 when implemented as a standalone unit [15]. The DES chip costs approximately $500.

There are three basic methods (see Figure 8-3) for using DES in a communications system [16]. The first is in the form of an electronic code book, in which, as described earlier, the plaintext 64-bit data block M is transformed to produce E. When the same key is used, the same ciphertext E is obtained each time M is encrypted, much like using a code book. The second method is cipher feedback, in which E_0 is produced from an initializing block, I_0, and then G_1 is produced by applying the transformation to E_0. E_1, corresponding to M_1 (the first data block to be encrypted) is produced by adding G_1 and M_1. The data blocks thus do not go through the DES transformation. The third method is block chaining, in which the data block M_2 is first added to the ciphertext E_1 from transforming data block M_1; the sum is then transformed in the DES device. In general, this method provides greater protection than do the other two.

Both the block-chaining and cipher-feedback methods are useful when encrypting serial data files for storage in direct-access devices or for stream-mode transmission. They are not as suitable for encrypting data in random-access memory units (RAMs), where each word must remain independently addressable, or for encrypting packets in a packet-switching data communications network, where packets may arrive out of sequence but must be decrypted immediately upon arrival. The electronic code book mode encryption is more suitable for these applications.

APPLICATIONS

The suitability of a class of encryption transformations for application in a data communications or file system depends on the relevant characteristics of

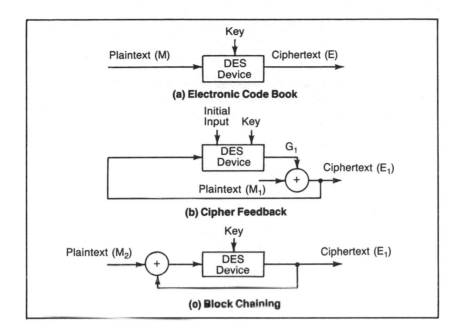

Figure 8-3. Principal Modes for Using the DES

the particular application, the inherent characteristics of the various classes of the selected transformations, and the technical aspects of the system. Although the purpose of encryption is to secure data in transit or storage, its effects on the utility of the application or system are equally important. A system might be designed to provide excellent security but at a loss in performance or ability to use such that it becomes practically worthless.

Application characteristics that affect the choice of encryption transformations include:

- The value of the information to be protected—Assessing the value of certain types of data (e.g., personal information) might be difficult, but risk analysis methods can provide assistance [6, 7]. Time dependence of the value is important—if the encryption transformation used can resist cryptanalytic attacks for T hours but the value of the information decreases below a critical threshold within this time, the selected transformation may provide adequate protection.
- The type of language used—Information in a message (or computer record) is expressed in a language characterized by a vocabulary, grammar, syntax, and certain statistical characteristics (e.g., the relative frequency of occurrence of different characters of the alphabet). If a natural language (one that has evolved over a long period of time) is used, its characteristics tend to be useful for cryptanalysis [17, 9, 16, 10]. When designing artificial languages (e.g., programming languages), the need for providing cryptographic protection can

be taken into account. Language characteristics can be designed to minimize their usefulness for statistical analysis.
- Dimensions and dynamics of the application—These characteristics include the volume of messages or records that must be transmitted or stored, required rates and response times, nature of processing to be performed, and error tolerances. These all establish a set of criteria that must be met by the cryptosystem used.

Resistance to Attack

The most important characteristic of an encryption transformation is its ability to resist cryptanalytic attacks or attempts to test all keys by force. The following types of attacks are usually considered:
- Statistical analyses of ciphertext, using language characteristics and testing hypotheses about possible keys or message content
- Attempts to determine the key used when the plaintext and corresponding ciphertext are available (the "known plaintext attack")
- Mathematical analyses of the transformation used and formulation of sets of equations that could produce the key on the basis of intercepted ciphertext

Correspondingly, the important intrinsic characteristics of cryptographic transformations are:
- Size of the key space—It must be very large in order to make trial-and-error attempts to find the key impractical.
- Effect of the transformation on language statistics—Ideally, such language characteristics as relative frequencies of single letters, pairs of letters (digraphs), and word structure should be completely masked and altered.
- Complexity—The transformation should be complex enough to prevent mathematical analysis and to multiply the time required for brute-force search. On the other hand, complexity affects the cost of application, in terms of both time and equipment used.
- Effect on dimensions—Such transformations as polygraphic substitutions of a character by a group of characters expand the length of ciphertext message over that of its plaintext. This affects transmission time and storage requirements.
- Error susceptibility—Simple substitutions are applied independently for each character; thus, no error propagation can occur. Errors in block product transformations and in cipher-feedback-mode operation propagate throughout the block or subsequent ciphertext.
- Length of the key—Keys shorter than the message must be applied several times cyclically in the encryption process. This provides assistance in cryptanalysis. Long keys generated by a pseudorandom process based on a few short parameters (as in random number generators) are also weak because the parameters (not the sequence) must be regarded as the true key. Systems that use randomly selected keys that are longer than the message and used only once are theoretically, as well as

practically, unbreakable [10]. Many keys must be available in active systems, and key generation, management, and security become serious problems.

- Synchronization—Such transformations as stream ciphers work only when the encryption/decryption devices are synchronized in time; both are in correct initial states when transmission begins and will remain so throughout the transmission. Loss of synchronization resulting from some error condition in the channel can prevent correct decryption. Block ciphers that do not use cipher feedback usually do not require time synchronization, but the beginning of the block must be clearly identified. The DES transformation has a self-synchronizing property even though an entire block may be lost when synchronization is lost. In general, the need for synchronization exposes the system to jamming attacks through deliberate insertion of noise into the communications link.

Simple monoalphabetic substitutions and transpositions do not hide language characteristics [18]. Polyalphabetic substitutions alter the single-character or digraph frequencies as a function of the length of the key (number of alphabets used). If the message is about 20 times as long as the key, computer-aided analysis can detect the language characteristics [11]. When higher-order statistics are also used, the difficulty of a statistical analysis attack is greatly reduced [19]. In messages or records expressed in artificial languages (e.g., programming or query languages), language statistics can be designed to be less revealing (e.g., all characters could have an equal frequency of use, all words could be the same length, and all possible words could be used). Numerical data is also secure against statistical analyses, especially when long sequences of leading zeros are removed prior to encryption. On the other hand, artificial languages tend to have more rigid formats and syntax and thus assist cryptanalysts.

Technical Considerations

Technical considerations in the application of cryptographic techniques include:
- Processing capability—This involves the availability of sufficiently high speed processors to perform the encryption/decryption operations within the time constraints of the application and without unduly degrading the channel transmission capability.
- Error environment—Error characteristics of the communications channel are important in choosing the encryption system. For example, in a highly error prone channel, using transformations that propagate errors or require continuous synchronization can lead to a great deal of wasted transmission resulting from the need to retransmit messages that could not be decrypted or to resynchronize the system.
- Operational environment—This consideration includes the type of system and its control as well as the training of system users and operators.

- Key distribution and management—Consideration should be devoted to the techniques used for key generation, distribution, and control. These techniques are crucial in determining the success of a cryptosystem but are often overlooked in the beginning.

These factors must all be taken into account by the data communications manager when considering encryption, particularly operator/user training. Experience has shown [9] that much of the success of cryptanalysts in breaking complex military and diplomatic cryptosystems can be directly associated with the improper security practices of systems users, including:

- Using the same key many times to transmit different messages when such practice is contrary to system requirements, thus allowing the cryptanalyst to hypothesize solutions and test them on several cipher-texts simultaneously
- Sending plaintext after failing several times to transmit the ciphertext without error
- Using highly formatted repetitive text in encrypted messages that can be easily guessed in relation to the context of the language or application used, thus providing a source of plaintext for the cryptanalyst
- Publishing a message verbatim that was transmitted earlier in encrypted form
- Using the same key for longer periods than specified for the given cryptosystem, thus providing material for cryptanalysis that is beyond what is considered acceptable by system designers
- Using an old key to send the new key, thus compromising the security of the new key

In general, despite rigid operational restrictions, a great many ciphertext and corresponding plaintext fragments might become available to interceptors/cryptanalysts. It is important, therefore, to use a cryptosystem that is as effective as possible in view of the application, system, performance, and cost. For example, if English text is to be transmitted, using the DES transformation would be superior to using stream ciphers based on polyalphabetic substitutions with relatively short keys. The latter, however, can be very effective in protecting numerical data.

There are practical considerations in introducing encryption into a system in a commercial environment [20]:

- Security in the system should depend on a minimum number of manual operations and personnel, thus limiting the number of people who must be cleared to handle encryption keys.
- Daily data terminal users and system operators should not handle keys or require special training to transmit encrypted messages.
- Data link control procedures and protocols and network control programs should not require major modifications when encryption is introduced.
- Data link throughput should not be reduced noticeably in the encrypted transmission mode, particularly in the case of artificially added redundancy (e.g., padding plaintext messages with random characters or using polygraphic substitutions).

- The encryption transformations should not produce and transmit character groups that are also used by the communications system to control data links, switches, and so on. Means must be implemented to filter out such forbidden character groups or, as a minimum precaution, to clearly identify the ciphertext portions of a transmission so that these character groups are ignored by the network control programs.

There are numerous considerations and requirements that may be affected in varying degrees by introducing security requirements (encryption in particular) or that affect the choice of encryption transformations. Approximately 35 such requirements are examined in reference 21.

KEY MANAGEMENT

It is apparent from the preceding discussion that the security provided by a cryptosystem depends on the security of the keys used. This is especially true for systems in which all details of the transformations used are public knowledge, such as those using DES. The problem is thus to generate, distribute, store, and apply keys in a secure manner. Some general principles have already been mentioned, such as minimizing the number of employees who are permitted to handle the keys. In addition, key management requirements for file systems differ from those for communications systems:

- In data communications, encryption and decryption are performed at remote locations; thus, two copies of the key are required. In a file system, both operations are performed at the same location.
- In a communications link, the message remains encrypted for a short period of time and is subject to interception only for this period of time. In a file system, encrypted records are at risk indefinitely.
- Changing keys is a simple process in a communications system; changing a key in a file system requires that all records be reprocessed with the new key.

These differences affect the handling of keys and the selection and use of cryptosystems in file as opposed to communications systems. In file systems, it is necessary to store keys in the system for long periods of time and use them frequently, which tends to weaken their security.

In systems where keys are handled automatically, increased emphasis must be placed on reliable identification and authentication of users and systems involved in the communications process. Networks of computers are an especially demanding environment for key management when many users wish to engage in end-to-end encrypted communication with each other or require secure communications when interacting with various systems in the network.

Link-by-Link Encryption. In link-by-link encryption systems, each link has a separate key that can be changed automatically each time a message is transmitted (or less frequently). The keys can be stored in a tamper-proof encryption device in a read-only memory that can be physically distributed to switching centers at required intervals. Key management in this system is relatively simple and secure. If headers of messages are not encrypted, switching centers do not require access to the decrypted message, and decryption and encryption for the next link can be processed within the device. At the receiving terminal, authentication of receiver identity must be required before the receiver is permitted access to the message. Standard identification/authentication techniques include using passwords or some individual characteristic (e.g., signature, fingerprint).

End-to-End Encryption. In end-to-end encryption, it is impractical for every subscriber to possess a separate key for every possible individual or system he may wish to communicate with at some time. Storing many keys securely is as difficult as keeping them updated. It has been suggested instead that a network security center be established for both identifying/authenticating users and systems and distributing keys for the desired communication sessions [22, 23]. For this purpose, a hierarchy of keys can be established: session, submaster, and master keys. Keys on the lowest level would protect the data; keys on the higher level would protect lower-level keys [24, 25]. There must also be a master key that is kept secure without encrypting. This key can be in the possession of the network security officer. This approach is based on the premise that the best way to provide key security is to encrypt the keys.

The network security system concept works as follows [22]:

1. A user (X) who wants to communicate over an encrypted channel with another user (Y) by using end-to-end encryption identifies and authenticates his terminal and himself to the network security center (NSC) and then requests a key for communicating with Y.
2. NSC verifies from its data base the authority of X to communicate with Y and then contacts Y and identifies/authenticates the terminal and individual using it.
3. NSC now uses its submaster key (which is not available to X or Y) to communicate with the two terminals to deliver a key for the communication between X and Y.
4. At the end of the communication, the session key is discarded.

This approach is quite promising for implementation in networks with large user communities. In smaller networks, more conventional key distribution approaches are appropriate (e.g., physical delivery of the keys to communicators who require end-to-end encryption). The key could be selected by referring to an identification number or code associated with each key. A nonsecure channel could then be used if there is confidence that the list of keys and their identification system have not been compromised.

MESSAGE AUTHENTICATION

Authentication of the veracity and source of digitally transmitted and stored messages is important in applications where legally binding agreements are made or funds disbursed through the use of communications systems.

Electronic funds transfer (EFT) systems and various interbank clearinghouse activities are examples. Recent advances in developing one-way and trapdoor functions have brought the achievement of such message authentication capability much closer to reality [13, 26, 27, 28, 29, 30].

In one-way functions, it is easy to apply the function to some variables but very difficult to apply the inverse of the function to the result in order to recover the original variables or find the inverse function. For example, it is easy to compute the sum of a given set of integers, but, given the sum, it is virtually impossible to determine what the original numbers were because there are so many numbers that can add up to the given value. Finding the roots of a very high order polynomial is another example. The first suggestions for the use of one-way functions were for secure storage of passwords in computer memory [28]. Instead of passwords themselves, the results of transforming the password by a function (F) were stored. Each time a password was submitted, F was evaluated and compared with the stored value. If they agreed, a correct password was used. Because the inverse F^{-1} is very difficult to compute, it did not matter if anyone gained access to the list of transformed passwords in the computer memory.

Functions in which both F and F^{-1} are easy to apply but F^{-1} is very difficult to find even if F is known have additional applications. An individual (X) can generate such a pair, F_X and F_X^{-1}, and make F_X public while keeping sole possession of its inverse F_X^{-1}. Then, anyone can send X a message by using F for encryption, but only X can decrypt it. A digital signature feature can now be implemented as follows. When X sends a message to party Y and wants to verify that it came from no one else, X first applies to message M_X the inverse transformation F_X^{-1}: $E_X = F_X^{-1}(M_X)$. The receiver Y now applies the publicly available transformation F_X to recover $M_X(F_X(F_X^{-1}[M_X]) = M_X)$. This message must be authentic because only X could have applied the first transformation, that is, F_X^{-1}. For added security, X could also use Y's transformation, F_Y, to encrypt E_X.

One class of such functions uses the difficulty level in factoring very large numbers (100 digits or more) into prime factors [26]. Its generation, however, is too complex for discusson in this chapter. Its primary disadvantage is that many multiplications are required because it involves representing M as an integer and raising it to a power that is at least a 100-digit number.

A function based on the so-called knapsack-packing algorithm has been developed. Because only addition and multiplication are involved in its use, the signature generation process is greatly accelerated. As with many ideas that are just beginning to emerge, no proof of the security or insecurity of the proposed signature functions has been produced.

CONCLUSION

Encryption is an effective security technique for data communications systems; its use has been greatly facilitated by the availability of the government-approved Data Encryption Standard. Current research in message authentication techniques may provide additional safeguards for the transmission of data. Accompanying the interest in developing new data encryption methods, however, is an almost certain equal interest in developing new ways to break them.

References

1. Parker, D.B. *Crime by Computer.* New York: Charles Scribner's Sons, 1976.
2. Allen, B. "Embezzler's Guide to the Computer." *Harvard Business Review* (July-August 1975) 79-89.
3. Linde, R.R. "Operating System Penetration." *Proceedings of the 1975 NCC,* 1975.
4. "Taps to Steal Data." *Security World* (December 1972) 45-46.
5. Carroll, J.M., and Reeves, P. "Security and Data Communications: A Realization of Piggy-Back Infiltration." *Infor* (October 1973) 226-231.
6. Courtney, R.H., Jr. "Security Risk Assessment in Electronic Data Processing Systems." *Proceedings of the 1977 NCC,* 1977.
7. Reed, S.K. *Automatic Data Processing Risk Assessment.* NBSIR 77-1228. Washington DC: National Bureau of Standards, March 1977.
8. Glaseman, S., Turn, R., and Gaines, R.S. "Problem Areas in Computer Security Assessment." *Proceedings of the 1977 NCC,* 1977.
9. Kahn, D. *The Codebreakers.* New York: Macmillan, 1967.
10. Shannon, C. "Communications Theory of Secrecy Systems." *Bell System Technical Journal* (October 1949) 654-715.
11. Tuckerman, B. *A Study of Vigenere-Vernam Single and Multiple Loop Enciphering Systems.* RC 2879. Yorktown Hts NY: IBM Thomas Watson Research Center, 1970.
12. *Data Encryption Standard.* FIPS PUB 46. Washington DC: National Bureau of Standards, January 1977.
13. Diffie, W., and Hellman, M.E. "New Directions in Cryptography." *IEEE Transactions on Information Theory* (November 1976) 644-654.
14. Diffie, W., and Hellman, M.E. "Cryptanalysis of the NBS Data Encryption Standard." *Computer* (June 1977) 74-84.
15. *Computer Security and the Data Encryption Standard.* Edited by D. Branstad. SP 500-27. Washington DC: National Bureau of Standards, February 1978.
16. Kent, S.T. "Network Security: A Topdown View Shows Problem." *Data Communications* (June 1978) 57-75.
17. Gaines, H.F. *Cryptanalysis.* New York: Dover Publications Inc, 1956.
18. Turn, R. "Privacy Transformations for Databank Systems." *Proceedings of the 1973 NCC,* 1973.
19. Tuchman, W.L., and Meyer, C.H. "Efficacy of the Data Encryption Standard in Data Processing." *Proceedings of 1978 Fall COMPCON,* 1978.
20. Schmid, P.E. "Review of Ciphering Methods to Achieve Communication Security in Data Transmission Networks." *Proceedings of the 1976 ICC,* 1976.
21. Shankar, K.S., and Chandersekaran, C.S. "The Impact of Security on Network Requirements." *Symposium Proceedings: Trends and Applications 1977 Computer Security and Integrity.* IEEE, 1977.
22. Branstad, D. "Encryption Protection in Computer Data Communications." *Proceedings of the Fourth Data Communications Symposium.* Quebec, Canada, 1975.
23. Heinrich, F. *The Network Security Center: A System Level Approach to Computer Network Security.* SP 500-21, Vol. 2. Washington DC: National Bureau of Standards, February 1978.
24. "Cryptography," *IBM Systems Journal,* No. 2, 1978.
25. Everton, J.K. "A Hierarchical Basis for Encryption Key Management in a Computer Communication Network." *Proceedings of the 1978 International Communications Conference,* Toronto, Canada, 1978.
26. Merkle, R.C. "Secure Communications in Insecure Channels." *Communications on the ACM* (April 1978) 294-299.
27. Merkle, R.C., and Hellman, M.E. "Hiding Information and Signatures in Trapdoor Knapsacks." *IEEE Transactions on Information Theory* (September 1978) 525-530.
28. Purdy, G.B. "A High-Security Log-In Procedure." *Communications of the ACM* (August 1974) 442-445.
29. Rivest, R.L., Shamir, A., and Adleman, L. "A Method for Obtaining Digital Signatures and Public Key Cryptosystems." *Communications of the ACM* (February 1978) 120-126.
30. Shamir, A. *A Fast Signature Scheme.* Department of Mathematics, Massachusetts Institute of Technology, Cambridge MA, May 1978.

Bibliography

Branstad, D., Gait, J., and Katzke, S. *Report of the Workshop on Cryptography in Support of Computer Security.* NBSIR 77-1291. Washington DC: National Bureau of Standards, September 1977.

Burris, H.R. "Computer Network Cryptography Engineering." *Proceedings of the 1976 NCC,* 1976.

Sinkov, A. *Elementary Cryptanalysis—A Mathematical Approach.* New York: Random House, 1968.

$\circledS$ Network Control Systems

by Gary Zielke

INTRODUCTION

The proliferation of data communications networks has brought with it an increased need for reliability and availability. Managers must now be capable of controlling network costs, evaluating network performance, and isolating and quickly restoring network failures. There are, fortunately, a number of tools to aid in accomplishing this task. In discussing the variety of available hardware that can be used to organize, monitor, and control network operations, this chapter provides essential information for planning and implementing a network management center.

PROVIDING EFFECTIVE CONTROL

Physical Organization

The first step in providing effective network control involves very little in the way of equipment and is applicable to even the smallest systems. It basically involves housing the communications equipment in or near the DP center, physically organized in such a way that existing equipment can be easily found and identified. Modems and other equipment should be kept in cabinets. Cabling should be organized and labeled (possibly coded by color) so that changes need not entail lengthy searches for the proper connecting pair. A diagram showing network locations, facilities, and equipment should be posted conspicuously and kept updated to assist anyone making repairs. Equipment manuals and operating instructions should be kept nearby in a secure place for quick consultation. Although these are commonsense items, they can, when overlooked, make even simple networks difficult to manage.

Diagnostic Equipment

The second step is to obtain basic diagnostic equipment and, depending on network size, line- and modem-patching capability.

Break-out Box. A low-cost and very useful piece of test equipment, a break-out box monitors and, if necessary, temporarily modifies the activity of

the RS-232C modem/terminal or modem/computer-port interface. Monitoring
the RS-232C interface status during operation can be compared with measuring
pulse rate and blood pressure. This equipment can quickly confirm the health of
a particular line, terminal, or modem and provide clues to the cause(s) of a
malfunction. With indicator lights on the front of most modems that display the
status of certain key interface leads, it is not always necessary to use the break-
out box to determine lead activity. A break-out box is, however, a good
investment, providing a more complete knowledge of RS-232C activity and the
ability to modify lead status for testing purposes.

Block-Error-Rate Tester. Another useful piece of test equipment is a bit-
or block-error-rate tester. With this device, users can test the error performance
of the lines and modems by transmitting a known bit pattern and then checking
it for errors. This type of test is disruptive, since it interrupts the normal data
flow. It can be done in end-to-end mode (requiring one unit at each end of the
circuit) or in loopback mode. The end-to-end test can determine the error
performance of a 2-wire line, or it can isolate errors as they occur on the
transmit or receive pair of a 4-wire line. The loopback test needs only one unit
but requires that the line at the remote end be turned around on itself. This
implies 4-wire or full-duplex 2-wire operation, as shown in Figure 9-1. Virtually all modems have loopback capability. Many have built-in bit-error-rate
testers, and certain break-out boxes also include this capability, making extra
equipment unnecessary. With these two pieces of equipment—the break-out
box and the bit-error-rate tester—many network problems can be quickly
isolated.

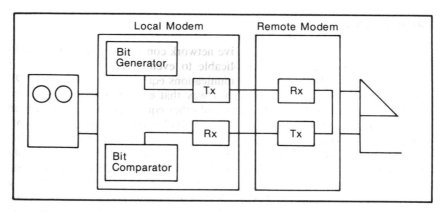

Figure 9-1. Digital Loopback Test

Patch Panel. When there are more than five or six modems at the central
site, some form of patching should be considered. A patch panel's primary
purpose is to facilitate rapid access to communications lines, modems, and
interface leads for testing, monitoring, and switching. (Figure 9-2 illustrates a
typical patching configuration.) For example, central-site personnel may wish
to switch a line to a different port to isolate a problem. The patch panel allows
them to do this without accessing the actual RS-232C interface cables. This

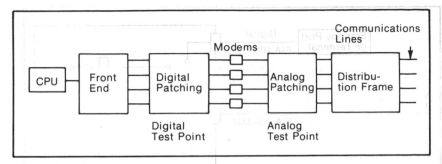

Figure 9-2. Digital and Analog Patching

ability becomes a significant advantage at a multiple-modem site because it eliminates the inconvenience of looking for the proper cable—and the likelihood of disturbing another connection in the process.

Because the access points for the monitoring or test equipment are at the front of the panel (rather than in the back with all the wiring), monitoring the communications line and the RS-232C interface is much easier. Even with modems located in several cabinets, most tests can be performed at a single console or cabinet where the patch panels are mounted. Both analog and digital patch panels are required. Analog patching connects the communications line to the modem; digital patching connects the modem and the computer or front end. Figure 9-3 is a schematic of a digital patch connection; one such connection would be required for every modem. Under normal conditions, the modem connects directly to its assigned computer port. When necessary, the modem can be changed by plugging a patch cable into the computer jack and plugging the other end into the new modem. This action simultaneously disconnects the existing modem and connects the new one, with no need to touch the actual wired connections. The monitoring connection allows test equipment (e.g., a break-out box) to be connected without disturbing the actual interface connection. Display lamps on some patch panels allow continuous monitoring of certain RS-232C interface leads so that the network operator can quickly check their status. Some digital patch panels also provide the ability to switch between ports on different front ends, quickly restoring service by bringing the standby unit online if one front end fails. The ability to make temporary patch connections is also available on the analog side of the modem. Figure 9-4 shows the corresponding connections of an analog patch panel.

Packaged Network Control Systems

The third step addresses the problem of accessing remote network locations to obtain status or diagnostic information. Because remote-site personnel are often nontechnical, it becomes difficult for central-site personnel to diagnose and remedy line and modem problems without visiting the site. One solution to this problem is the use of packaged network control systems, which are available from several modem vendors.

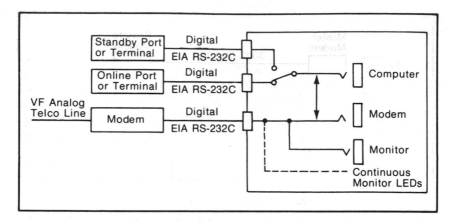

Figure 9-3. Digital Patch Panel

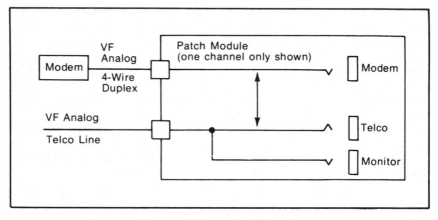

Figure 9-4. Analog Patch Panel

Each central-site and remote modem is equipped with an optional circuit card that allows the network controller to perform various monitoring, testing, and switching functions. Every few seconds, a central-site control unit sequentially polls each modem on the line to obtain status and/or alarm information. (Signaling uses a supervisory channel [see Figure 9-5] so that the main data stream is not affected.) A lack of response or a parameter not within specification generates an alarm at the central site, identifying the time, location, and nature of the trouble for remedial action. A typical alarm condition is modem streaming, which occurs when one of the remote modems on a multipoint circuit does not turn off its carrier signal after data transmission. Because all remote modems share the same line in a multipoint circuit, no other modem/terminal can respond. The problem is particularly disruptive because central-site personnel cannot easily determine which modem is causing the problem. Someone at each remote location must be called and asked to check whether the request-to-send/clear-to-send (RTS/CTS) leads are on.

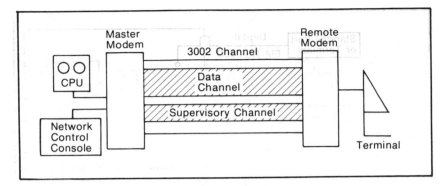

Figure 9-5. Network Control Systems

After explaining to the remote-site personnel what they must look for, the problem is usually cleared by disconnecting the modem or terminal power.

With remote diagnostics systems, a time limit for carrier-signal duration can be set at each site. Exceeding this time limit sends an alarm to the central site through the side channel, which is unaffected by the streaming. Some systems also automatically shut off the streaming modem so that the remainder of the line will continue to function without central-site operator intervention. Other conditions that can trigger alarms (depending on the system) include various analog parameters, signal quality, loss of data terminal ready, and one or more external events (e.g., room temperature at the remote site). A sensor capable of closing a contact at a given temperature could be connected to the remote modem. Exceeding this predetermined value would cause the modem to detect the contact closure, setting off the appropriate alarm at the central site.

Network control systems also allow central-site personnel to observe the status of the RS-232C interface and certain analog parameters remotely and without affecting service. If a remote site complains of higher-than-normal errors, the central site can quickly and nondisruptively check the signal quality and analog parameter(s) by selecting the remote modem at a control console. If this test reveals that given parameters have drifted off their normal setting, a call can be placed to the carrier, suggesting what the problem might be. If the test proves inconclusive, other tests can also be performed from the central site. Although most of these tests are disruptive, they can usually be done quickly to minimize downtime. Such tests include the following:

- Modem self-test—This causes the questioned modem to perform a set of predetermined diagnostics on itself. If the test is successful, the modem is probably not at fault; failure indicates that the modem most likely is at fault.
- Bit-error-rate test—These tests (similar to those described earlier) can isolate errors in the transmit or receive line or the modem.
- Poll test—This special kind of bit-error-rate test simulates the polling and responses on a multipoint line. This test occasionally reveals problems undetected by a steady-state error test.

Once the problem has been identified, the packaged network control systems allow central-site personnel to initiate restoral procedures. If uptime is extremely important, one or more remote sites may include backup equipment. A faulty remote modem can be replaced with the hot standby modem via command from the central site; a suspect line can also be replaced automatically with a backup circuit. Primarily because of cost, dedicated lines are often backed up with dial-up lines. Because most dedicated lines operate in 4-wire mode and dial-up lines are restricted to two wires, two dial-ups are required for each site to be backed up, with a matching set of two at the central site. Backup then requires placing two dial calls and switching both ends from the dedicated to the switched connection. Much of this can be done automatically, depending on the sophistication of the system.

It is sometimes possible to solve a line problem temporarily by operating the modems at a lower speed while awaiting carrier response to the trouble call. If the modems have this speed-fallback capability, some network control systems allow this feature to be invoked on all affected modems from the central site.

A printer can often be attached when a hard-copy record of status checks and trouble or alarm events is required. Some systems can be programmed to perform predetermined tests (usually nondisruptive) at specified time periods and record the results. Slowly degrading conditions can thus be detected before a total failure occurs. (This is often called predictive diagnostics, a subject discussed further in a later section of this chapter.)

Wraparound systems that provide many of the remote testing and control features already described are available for organizations with a considerable investment in existing modem equipment. It is generally more desirable to purchase modems and test equipment as a package since a network control system that is designed to work with a particular modem series usually offers more features than do others.

This, however, is not always possible or economically feasible, so a wraparound system is ideal for organizations wishing to use the remote testing and control features without replacing modems. The wraparound system is so named because it interfaces with an existing modem on both the line and the RS-232C sides—surrounding the modem electrically. It can therefore perform some (but usually not all) of the tests and controls of integral systems.

Alternatives

Two other classes of equipment can be considered in addition or as an alternative to packaged network control systems: data line monitors and analog test sets.

Data Line Monitors. Data line monitors allow users to observe the flow of data on both the transmit and receive pins of the RS-232C interface. In addition, these units can often monitor the status of all RS-232C leads, timing events such as RTS/CTS delay, recording the data flow on tape, flagging specific data sequences, and emulating data terminal equipment.

The value of a data line monitor is best described by an example. Protocol and/or timing problems often appear as line errors, as in the case of a multi-point polled line. The CPU starts a timer each time it sends out a poll. If the terminal does not respond within a predetermined interval, the CPU assumes a problem and polls again or goes on to the next terminal. If the time-out value, based on the propagation delay of the line, is too short, the terminal's normal response may appear as garbled data; in such a case, the CPU has gone on and has tried to poll the next terminal. Bit-error-rate tests and modem and terminal self-tests would all check out, leaving the user with the contradiction of negative tests and a remaining problem. By actually seeing the data flow, the user could observe that issuing a new poll during receipt of the previous message caused the garble. Knowledge of the protocol and terminal operation would indicate a time-out problem, and the time-out parameter could then be reset to a larger value.

Because of the number of available models with a wide range of capabilities and prices, selection of the appropriate unit is a nontrivial exercise. Prospective users must be familiar with their network configurations and needs before purchasing so that an appropriate model is selected. It is also helpful for the first-time purchaser to check with other users to determine the most useful features. Although the data line monitor is a powerful and invaluable instrument for isolating protocol and/or time-out problems, it cannot be used effectively without knowledge of the line protocol and the terminals.

Analog Test Sets. Analog line testing and monitoring also require some user sophistication to be beneficial. In many cases, digital tests are sufficient to indicate that the problem is modem, terminal, or line related. The normal procedure for a line problem is to call the carrier. If the problem is resolved, normal operation continues. If no trouble is found and the problem persists, however, additional action is required. One approach is to use more sophisticated digital tests, such as those possible with a data line monitor. Another approach is to perform analog line tests (similar to those performed by the carrier) to confirm or challenge the carrier's results. This second approach requires specialized analog test equipment and training.

Analog lines are subject to a number of transmission impairments that can singly or in combination contribute to unsatisfactory data transmission; the more common of these impairments include:

- Transmission loss—the circuit's end-to-end loss in signal strength measured at a specific frequency (1,000 Hz)
- Amplitude distortion—the variations in end-to-end circuit loss as a function of signal frequency (sometimes called frequency response)
- Message or steady-state noise—background electrical noise (introduced by various factors) affecting the intelligibility of the data signal (analogous to office background noise caused by equipment, air conditioning, or outside traffic)
- Impulse or transient noise—high-amplitude short-duration noise often caused by various types of switching
- Envelope delay distortion—impairment caused by a nonlinear relationship between data signal frequency and phase, caused by filters and

transmission-line characteristics
- Nonlinear or harmonic distortion—caused by the introduction of frequencies that are multiples of the data signal frequencies (often a result of using a compander to improve the quality of voice transmission)

Although improvements in analog test equipment make it easier for nontechnical people to perform the necessary tests, measurement is only part of the answer. The information must be communicated to the carrier's maintenance staff. If the carrier's test results are being challenged, it is strongly suggested that the person communicating this information have some appropriate technical background. Otherwise, credibility may be a problem. Carrier personnel may show resentment, feeling that analog testing infringes on their domain. Tact and diplomacy are essential if analog testing is to be useful.

Analog testing, however, does not solve the problem; it is merely an aid to isolating the cause of the trouble. In this regard, user and carrier personnel should function as a team, recognizing that it is less important who isolates the fault than that it is discovered—and remedied.

DIGITAL NETWORKS

The use of digital lines in a data communications network requires some variations to the methods described previously. Clearly, analog tests are unnecessary when the carrier provides a time-division-multiplexed digital channel operating at a fixed speed, as opposed to a frequency-division-multiplexed analog channel. Data service units (DSUs), the modem-like devices that interface to the data terminal equipment, are usually supplied by the carrier, who performs most or all loopback testing. Some RS-232C status information is displayed on the DSU. Remote units, however, cannot be monitored from the central site because these devices are generally not supported by packaged network control systems.

Because digital lines are not available everywhere, it is common to use a digital circuit from the central site to a remote digital serving area, with an analog tail circuit to the actual user site. Under these circumstances, it is possible (although difficult) to monitor and control the analog portion at the central site. The packaged network control systems require a low-speed channel over which the signaling information can be transmitted between the central site and the analog tail circuit. This is not a feature of Digital Dataphone Service (AT&T's digital network offering) and requires an additional level of multiplexing. A remote master control unit is also required; this would sit at the remote end of the digital circuit. Because operation of network control systems over digital networks is cumbersome and rather limited, most vendors of this equipment do not recommend operation in this mode. Potential users must therefore decide whether to go all analog and take advantage of the packaged system features or to go with digital service and rely more heavily on the carrier for trouble isolation.

CONCLUSION

Effective network management requires more than simply monitoring and controlling the network's availability and reliability. Performance must be monitored as well. Performance measurement has traditionally been done manually or in the communications software. It was, and frequently still is, measured by timing the response experienced at a terminal with a stopwatch.

Equipment now available provides various degrees of automated performance measurement, independent of the communications software. This offers the network manager an alternative to customizing communications software that lacks an acceptable performance measuring capability.

At the low end are response-time monitors that attach to individual terminals and provide performance statistics for a single device, while more sophisticated units can determine response-time performance for an entire line. Still others not only record response time but measure error performance and CPU delay; they also generate summary reports for information and action. Such capabilities provide the network manager with a very powerful tool for determining trends and the need for upgrades or redesign. It also becomes possible to confirm or dispute end-user claims of inadequate performance.

Utopia for a network manager may seem to be the ability to detect potential line or equipment problems and correct them before they cause a hard failure or become noticeable to end users. In the real world, however, the network manager generally finds out about a problem from the end user. The current generation of test and monitoring equipment does provide the manager with some predictive ability. Not all network failures can be predicted, of course, because some occur quickly and without warning. Many conditions, however, begin with slow degradation and eventually produce a hard failure. These latter conditions lend themselves to predictive diagnostics. Some of the more sophisticated test and control systems now available can be programmed to perform specific tests, such as measuring the analog line signal level, at regular intervals. During a period of several days, for example, the line signal level may be observed to be steadily decreasing. This could alert the network manager to a trend that should be corrected before it causes failure. Equipment or facilities that exhibit gradual degradation should be scheduled for off-hour maintenance so that end users are not aware of the repair and experience no downtime.

10 Disaster Recovery Planning

by Thomas J. Murray

INTRODUCTION

The increasing use of computer systems and the proliferation of data communications networks have led to greater management understanding of the need for a realistic disaster plan. The data communications manager must be involved in such planning and should be knowledgeable in the following areas:

- The need for disaster planning
- The various computer backup facility approaches
- The methods of evaluating these approaches
- The characteristics of a disaster backup network
- The available backup network design strategies
- The planning process(es) within the firm
- The organizational impact within the firm

This chapter discusses these important aspects of disaster planning and provides some background material. The information presented here is based on experience gained at SUNGARD™, a disaster recovery service of Sun Information Services Company, Philadelphia and Chicago.

THE DISASTER PLANNING PROCESS

The disaster planning process is no different from any other planning activity: goals, objectives, strategies, and implementation plans must be developed, and the plan coordinator must rely on line organizations to provide the necessary input. Disaster planning is complicated by the number of often intangible variables; it is also complicated because it generally involves, at some point, all departments within the firm. In some respects, it is similar to environmental forecasting at the corporate planning level. Producing an effective disaster plan requires significant organizational skill.

The initial question arising from the first meeting of the disaster planning team might be: What constitutes a disaster for the firm? The second might be: What functions and applications must we back up? Neither of these questions is trivial, and neither will be answered in the first meeting. For a firm whose computer center is situated near a busy airport, top management's prime phobia may be an air disaster; however, an ineffective maintenance program or a disgruntled employee's actions may make an extended hardware outage a more significant threat. Regarding the second question, there are techniques by which the critical nature of functions and specific applications can be evaluated and priorities established.

Whatever the situation, however, a disaster plan's objective is to permit the firm to react to the failure of the corporate data center in a structured manner that will minimize downtime and resultant losses. Since such a disaster and the subsequent recovery process involve and affect many aspects of the firm's operations, the planning and recovery processes are best implemented through the management team concept. This concept involves forming a managerial team that represents all major functional areas, supported by their respective line organizations. Such functional areas might include financial analysis, communications, systems software, application software, operations, hardware, facilities development, logistics support preparation, and data control. The major departments and divisions of the firm (as users and decision makers) should also be represented. To be effective, disaster planning requires the direction and participation of top management, since many decisions will require this level of attention.

The data communications manager is an important member of this team for several reasons. The author's experience in this area indicates that the backup network issue often becomes a key factor in decisions concerning the firm's level of commitment to disaster planning. This is mainly because of the complexities and perceived high costs of backup networks. Communications backup is often believed to be a major obstacle to the successful implementation of a recovery plan; however, backup networks can and are being implemented successfully at reasonable costs, using some of the strategies discussed in this chapter.

The data communications manager will be asked to supply a disaster backup network plan that deals with critical applications and the backup methodology. This is often an iterative process in that the data communications manager may be asked to provide several alternatives of a backup network design, depending on the backup methodology used. It is important to note that the methodology chosen to counteract a disaster affects the backup network design and the number and types of critical applications to be backed up.

The Need for Disaster Planning

Given the complexities of disaster planning, is it wise for management to spend considerable time and resources in developing a corporate disaster plan? Although the probabilities of any computer center or data network being destroyed may be relatively small, the conditional expectant loss to the firm in such an event can be staggering. Disasters can and will continue to happen (see references 1 and 2). Exact statistics are difficult to obtain; actual disasters are not well publicized, in order to maintain the integrity of the firm's operations. The it-can't-happen-here attitude should be avoided and the problem approached as a business decision.

To assist in this decision, some consultants have a risk analysis program available that can calculate annual expected losses for each critical business operation and each type of disaster situation. It is hoped in this way to provide guidelines for resource allocation of countermeasures. Because major disasters have a low probability of occurrence, the analysis must be conducted rigorously. The expectant loss, mathematically, is the product of the financial losses caused by the disaster and the probability of occurrence of the disaster, possibly making this value deceptively low. It should be noted that the expectant loss is also a function of outage time. Perhaps what should also be considered is the conditional probability of excessive financial loss—the probability of business failure when a particular disaster occurs. This might be used as a weight in such an analysis. The disaster phenomenon is somewhat analogous to a firm's inability to cope with a drastic change in its environment. There has been such an unfortunate occurrence recently in the domestic automobile industry.

A study [3] conducted by the University of Minnesota's Graduate School of Business Administration examined a cross-section of various industries, with informative results. It was found that there is a nonlinear (almost exponential) decline in operational business activities as the disaster continues. Typically, within one week—and for some industries, within a few days—of a data center failure, most automated business activities cease to function. Financial losses then rapidly accumulate almost exponentially. The study helped to verify the following important points:
- It is important to minimize the duration of the outage in order to minimize the financial losses (which build up rapidly).
- Automated business functions typically cease operation within one week after an outage.
- The value of this variable depends on the type of industry.

One of the parameters in controlling outage time is the backup methodology; another is the presence and effectiveness of the disaster plan in using the chosen methodology.

COMPUTER FACILITY BACKUP APPROACHES

There are several basic methods of backing up a computer center [4, 5, 6, 7, 8]:
- Passive approach
- Buy time—application backup
- Mutual aid, agreements for computer time
- Empty shell or ready space
  - Cooperative approach
  - Company owned
  - Vendor-supplied service

- Second center—company-owned center integrated into the normal production environment
- Fully equipped recovery center
  - Company owned
  - Cooperative venture
  - Vendor-supplied service

The effect each method will have on the backup network design must be considered. As the firm becomes more involved in disaster planning, each method can be evaluated by answering at least the following questions:

- What is the cost of the method? How much is the firm willing to pay?
- How quickly can the firm be operational with the method? What is the longest outage the firm can withstand? How well does the method minimize the outage time?
- How reliable is the method? What reliability is required for guaranteed access to the facility, compatibility of hardware and software, and required capacity?

The communications manager should, of course, be involved in answering these questions, since the backup network design affects cost, reliability, and access time.

Passive Approach. With the passive approach, the firm does not attempt to do anything special. It simply waits for the expeditious delivery of hardware, software, and physical facilities. The communications manager will be required to explore the possibilities of accelerating the normal ordering/ delivery schedule with each vendor. In addition, if the existing facilities are not usable, the network must be transferred to the new facilities. This approach implies a crisis mode of planning, and the firm must expect a lengthy outage caused by low reliability.

Application Backup. The second approach assumes that selected critical applications will be backed up by an agreement between the firm and a vendor who will supply the remote computing services. Depending on the access time required and the desire to test such services periodically (if possible), it may be necessary to have a limited backup network in place. For large online data base applications, implementing this method could be difficult.

Mutual Aid Agreement. The mutual aid agreement is usually with a firm in the same geographic area that has similar DP requirements. One company agrees to provide backup facilities for another company and vice versa. For the communications manager, this may require installing backup facilities at the other organization's center, possibly including front-end processors, modems, and circuit terminations as required. The other company, of course, may desire to do the same, but this depends on the configurations and access time anticipated. The tendency here is to accept gentlemen's agreements or best efforts to supply hardware at the other site, since mutual aid agreements are typically not enforceable. Although the implicit assumption is that there is always adequate spare capacity on both systems, this is generally not so.

Compounding this factor is the constant change in both systems. Most experts agree that this method should be considered only for limited, critical batch-oriented applications.

Empty Shell. The empty shell, or ready space, approach addresses the problem of a complete loss of the data center's physical facilities by providing a backup facility in an alternative location that has some conditioned space but no computer equipment. The shell may be company owned, or it may be provided by either a cooperative of many firms sharing the costs or a vendor. The facility would typically include the required power, air conditioning, and chilled water systems needed to support the computer and its peripherals. The assumption implicit in this approach is that all equipment can be received and installed in a timely manner, with a total outage time not exceeding what the firm can reasonably withstand. If a firm's maximum acceptable outage time were 48 hours, such an approach would be unacceptable.

The backup network required for this approach may already be in place, or it may be installed concurrently with the computer and peripheral equipment. This depends on the total time estimated, from when the disaster occurs to when the computer and peripherals can be operational. If this estimate compares favorably with the communications equipment vendors' and common carrier's lead times, plans should be made for standing orders to alleviate the paperwork delay. If the comparison is unfavorable, then the backup network, or part of it, must be in place at the shell. Another important factor for the shell is to ensure an adequate number of cable entrance facilities from the local telephone company. In some cases, ensuring that enough facilities are available may require payment of a monthly fee to reserve cable pairs.

Second Center. Another option is to set up a second computer center, which would be integrated into the production network. Each such center would be designed with sufficient spare capacity to process the critical backup load from the failed center. Each center must also remain compatible with all other centers. If this compatibility can be maintained, a firm can minimize its financial loss extremely well. Because the resultant access time is short, the communications network must be switched to the alternate center within the same time period. This backup concept may require a complete redesign of the production network, possibly converting to a nodal architecture with user-initiated switching capabilities to either center (these requirements depend on the size of the backup network). Because of the shorter access time (compared with the shell approach), vendors and carriers cannot realistically be expected to supply the backup communications needs. Whatever form the backup network takes, with the second center option, it must be in place prior to the disaster. This approach also requires substantial ongoing planning and monitoring to ensure that the spare capacity and compatibility are maintained.

Recovery Center. The last alternative considered here is that of a fully equipped second center used strictly for backup. If this center is provided by the firm itself, it may elect to run noncritical developmental work to help defray the sizable costs involved. Such a center might also be provided through a cooperative group of firms sharing the cost of the facility; however, based on historical evidence, a compromise configuration would be provided at best. The communications manager can expect extensive involvement in determining the common communications requirements of the group members and how best to use the facility. Another approach to this type of facility is the use of a vendor-supplied disaster backup service. Currently, only a few vendors supply such services, and they vary greatly in the manner in which they respond to backup network needs. The communications manager will have to evaluate how each vendor meets the needs of the firm's backup network. This process is discussed in a later section of this chapter.

It is thus apparent that the required access time is an important issue in both the backup network design and the selection of a suitable backup approach. There are, of course, other key characteristics.

Characteristics of a Disaster Backup Network

A disaster backup network must have certain characteristics, including:
- Reliability
- Operability
- Activation response time
- Cost-effectiveness

Reliability. In designing disaster recovery networks, regardless of the computer facility backup approach used, the organization must be confident that the network will function when and as required. This can be accomplished by using proven technology and standard tariffed offerings of the common carriers, which in turn permits a better understanding of the network operation. Since the network designer or other technically skilled personnel may not be available when a disaster occurs, keeping the design simple is a good idea. The use of informal gentlemen's agreements in this area is not recommended since critical components in the network design may be unavailable when required.

It should also be possible to test the backup network without seriously disrupting the production network. Disaster planning experts concur that a disaster plan is suspect without the ability to test it. Backup approaches such as the fully equipped center permit this testing; others, such as the shell, do not. Both application-oriented and limited testing should be performed, as should occasional full-load testing.

Operability. The network should be easily operated. Operability implies that the methods used for the backup design should be consistent with the production network environment. Simple procedures should outline the steps required to implement the backup network for each critical terminal. The ability to test provides operating personnel and end users with first-hand experience in implementing the network changeover. The backup network design and the operating procedures should be well documented and distributed to the proper personnel.

Activation Response Time. As previously mentioned, the backup network must be activated within the time constraints imposed by the computer facility backup method. Activation may be required for periodic testing (if the method permits). Most backup facilities are interim facilities in that the firm will operate there until the stricken facility is renovated or a new center built. The network design must be flexible in order to meet all these time-sensitive considerations.

Cost-Effectiveness. The backup network design (as with any other network design) should be cost-effective. There are major differences, however, in the design philosophies of the backup network and the daily production network. Since the backup network is usually idle, it is desirable to minimize the idle-state cost. If testing is available through the backup facility, a less-than-optimum network is permissable since testing periods are short and infrequent. In disaster operation, a less-than-optimum design is also permissable, since the important criterion is fast activation of the network, and the backup network will generally be operated on an interim basis until the permanent location is established. The disaster network should, however, be readily convertible for long-term use at the permanent site.

Backup Network Design Strategies

The importance of determining the critical applications to be backed up cannot be overstated. What is being discussed is the development of a plan that will allow a firm to recover from a disaster of such magnitude that failure to do so will seriously jeopardize the firm financially. Several recent surveys concerning disaster planning indicate that companies have, for the most part, tried to back up every application. This effort escalates the cost of backup, sometimes so much so that no measures are taken to protect the firm.

A number of methods can be used for determining the critical applications [8, 9]. The basic analysis should consider each application and its economic impact (from both an income and a cash-flow viewpoint) on the firm as a function of how long its processing is delayed. Each application should be identified as to its processing requirements, interdependencies, manual backup capability, type of hardware and software required, data preparation and control requirements, and scheduling requirements. The dollar losses caused by delays in processing the application can be entered into a matrix, listing the application system name as rows and the processing delay times as columns. Economic losses entered into the matrix might include such estimates as lost or delayed billings and accounts receivables, interest penalties, discount losses, additional costs of manual operation or operational inefficiencies, legal penalties, and losses caused by ill will. The effects of negative cash flows and credit ratings should also be estimated and noted in the matrix. Since many disaster recovery schemes provide limited processing capabilities immediately after a disaster, using the matrix permits critical applications to be scheduled and recovery facilities gradually upgraded in the required time.

Eliminating the terminals used for noncritical applications provides a subset of terminals for which the disaster backup network design is required. In addition, the matrix can assist in developing the critical work load for each terminal as well as the timing relationships during which the work load increases from the critical to the normal value. This knowledge is essential because the firm must eventually phase in normal operations after a disaster. The communications manager can then use the following strategies to further reduce the number of terminals:

- Investigate combining the work loads of co-located terminals to minimize the total number of communications links required.
- Consider such cost-effective alternatives to data transmission as mail, air freight, courier, and company aircraft.
- Investigate the required terminal bandwidth, based on the elimination of the noncritical or developmental portion of the work load and on the use of an extended schedule during the recovery process.
- For online systems, investigate the acceptability of increasing response-time criteria to permit more terminals per line or the use of lower line speeds.
- Examine the possibilities for scheduled nonsimultaneous sharing of disaster backup communications facilities at the recovery site by taking advantage of time zone changes, staggered operation shifts, and overtime. Many batch terminals and even online terminals, for example, can share a common facility by accessing the facility only at prescheduled time periods.

BACKUP NETWORK DESIGN TECHNIQUES

Knowing the number of critical terminals and having a work load profile for each permits the application of backup network design techniques. It is important for the planner to have some knowledge of these techniques so that a practical implementation plan can be formulated from the disaster recovery plan. The backup technique varies, depending on how the critical terminal is configured on the production network. Most of the basic methods described in this section are currently in use.

Dial Access Terminals

For dial access terminals, which generally use the public dial-up network to access a hunt group in a computer center, the backup design consists simply of an alternate telephone number(s) and a duplicate set of dial access modems at the recovery site. For terminals that access a value-added carrier's packet network, a duplicate node may be required at the recovery site, or the public dial network could be used. A lower level of availability here may be adequate, requiring a smaller node size or fewer channels in the hunt group at the recovery site. Scheduled rather than random access can also reduce the number of channels required.

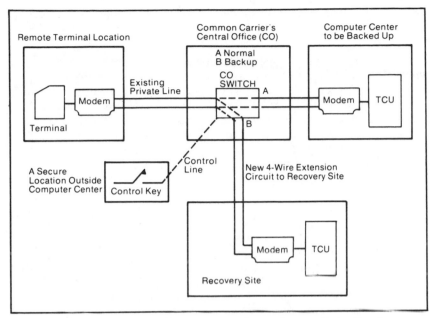

Figure 10-1. Circuit Extension Technique for a Point-to-Point Circuit

Point-to-Point Private-Line Analog Circuits

Three methods are available to provide a viable backup for point-to-point private-line circuits. The first method requires a circuit extension approach, and the second requires the use of 4-wire dial backup. The third method, which can be used when the critical work loads are small, uses an auxiliary 2-wire dial access modem.

Figure 10-1 is a functional diagram of the circuit extension technique, which is accomplished by installing a new 4-wire circuit from the local carrier's central office for each existing line to be backed up. Each new circuit is connected as an alternate drop on the existing point-to-point circuit by way of a 4-wire circuit switch, such as the Bell System's Western Electric Company (WECO) 29A. This switch, which is a tariffed offering for an AT&T Long Lines circuit, is located in the central office. (For other carriers and local Bell companies, it is usually a special assembly.) In one position, the activated switch permits data transmission to and from the recovery site; in the other position, it permits the passage of data to the data center, blocking the connection to the recovery site. This is an important security consideration when using a shared center or service bureau.

The switch is activated by a control line and a key located at a secure location other than the data center. Ganging switches, if desired, allows throwing one key to disconnect all associated circuits from the present data center and activating the extensions to the recovery site. If the recovery methodology permits periodic testing, smaller switch groupings are recommended to facilitate testing a smaller number of lines. It is also a good idea to test the extension circuit prior to the disaster test to ensure that the circuit is in service.

A less costly backup alternative for a point-to-point circuit is to use the 4-wire dial backup approach shown in Figure 10-2. This requires the installation of 4-wire dial backup facilities at each remote location and the recovery site, which also requires the installation of the appropriate modem. Scheduling access to the recovery site can significantly reduce the number of dial backup facilities and modems required at the recovery site. (The remote-site dial backup facilities can protect the production network from circuit failures, if dial backup facilities are also provided at the present data center.)

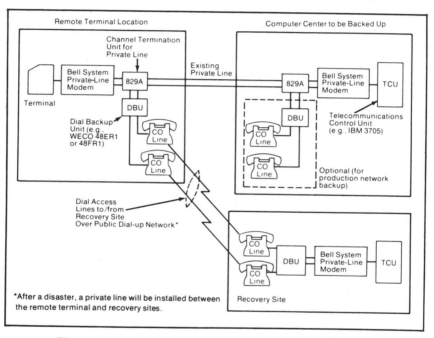

Figure 10-2. Dial Backup Technique for Point-to-Point Circuits

The dial backup facility for the Bell system private-line modems consists of adding a feature to the 829A channel termination arrangement and installing two central office telephone lines, as shown in Figure 10-2. For non-Bell private-line modems, the dial backup arrangement (see Figure 10-3) generally consists of two central office telephone lines, two FCC-registered data access arrangements (DAA), and a vendor-supplied dial backup switch. The DAAs are available from many manufacturers, and the dial backup switch is generally available from a non-Bell modem manufacturer.

The Bell dial backup unit is provided in two versions: WECO 48ER1 or 48FR1. The 48FR1 is a special unit operating solely in automatic-answer mode, while the 48ER1 can be used manually or automatically. For non-Bell

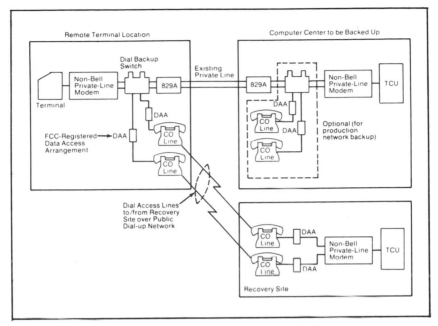

Figure 10-3. Dial Backup Technique for Non-Bell Modems

modems, some manufacturers also have automated versions for unattended dial backup operation. These units must all be FCC registered for direct connection to the public dial network through registered DAAs, or the unit itself must be registered.

As shown in Figures 10-2 and 10-3, the dial backup approach necessitates placing two calls: one for the transmit signal path, the other for the receive signal path. Once these connections are made, operation is similar to that of a private line. No changes need be made in the teleprocessing software required at the recovery site or in the terminal configuration.

Available studies of the performance of the dial backup arrangement indicate that in a high percentage of call attempts, the typical 9,600-bit-per-second modem achieves a significantly greater net throughput on a 4-wire dial backup connection, operating at 9,600 bits per second, than at its available, less error-susceptible 4,800-bit-per-second alternate rate. Since the 9,600-bit-per-second modem can also be used in multiplexing applications, many modems have a switch that prevents the modem from switching to a lower-speed alternate rate. A precautionary note: in suburban or rural areas where central office facilities have not been modernized, the use of 4-wire dial backup may be restricted to the lower speeds. A bit and block error-rate performance test may be required, in some cases, to verify the connection's use to the recovery site.

One advantage of the dial backup approach is that in case of disaster, the dedicated lines can be reterminated to the recovery site, using the same

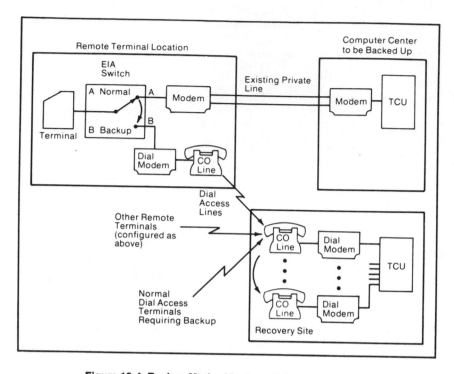

Figure 10-4. Backup Method for Low-Volume Terminals

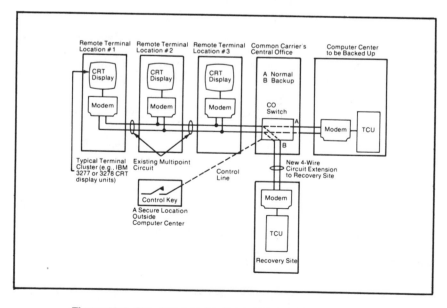

Figure 10-5. Circuit Extension Backup for Multipoint Circuits

modems. This means dial backup would only be used until the carrier could perform the retermination. Although no guarantees will be given (nor should be expected), past performance shows that the carriers generally do expedite these orders. Two additional factors can help ensure this. First, the required local cable entrance facilities should be available at the recovery site. (The local loop is already installed at the remote terminal site.) Second, the details of these new circuit orders should be thoroughly discussed with the carrier as part of the backup and recovery plan.

The last approach for point-to-point lines can be used when the critical work load is low and when the remote terminal can be easily modified to provide a dial access protocol. This approach, shown in Figure 10-4, uses a 2-wire dial access modem and a hunt group at the recovery site.

Multipoint Private-Line Analog Circuits

There are also three alternatives for multipoint circuits, which typically have clusters of online CRT terminals. The first uses the circuit extension technique already discussed. In the typical configuration shown in Figure 10-5, the new circuit extension to the recovery site would be connected as an alternate master station drop on the existing multipoint line via the carrier-

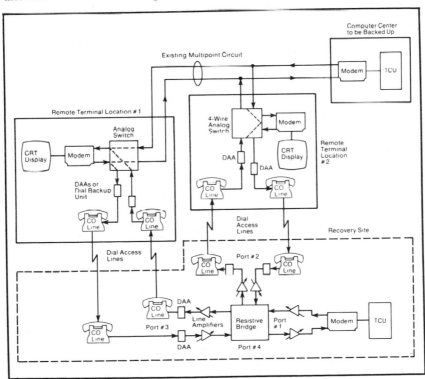

Figure 10-6. Backup for Multipoint Circuits Using Dial Backup and Data Bridge

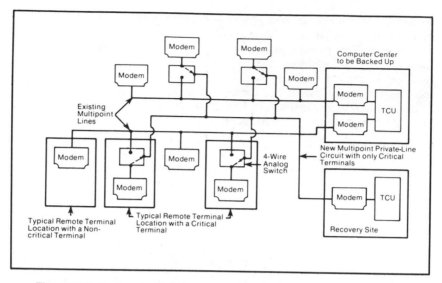

Figure 10-7. Backup for Multipoint Circuits Using a New Multipoint Circuit

supplied 4-wire switch in the central office. No changes are required in the teleprocessing software, and every terminal on the circuit is backed up.

A second method of backing up multipoint circuits implements 4-wire dial backup facilities at each critical drop on the multipoint circuit. This approach uses a data bridge at the recovery site, as shown in Figure 10-6. Each remote terminal places two dial backup calls to a port on the bridge. Once all connections have been made, the configuration appears the same to the teleprocessing software as the multipoint line configuration.

This approach requires careful consideration for several reasons—for example, the types of bridges used. One type of bridge is termed passive; that is, it has manually adjustable line amplifiers in each port of the bridge that adjust the receive levels to those required by the modems. The input and output levels of the bridge must also be consistent on all ports to keep the bridge in balance. If the drops are geographically dispersed, the received dial backup levels will vary because of the variance in the public dial network's loss, which is also time dependent. This required level adjustment can be cumbersome. An alternative is to use an active bridge, which provides automatic gain control in each port of the bridge.

Another reason for caution is that depending on the distances involved between the remote terminal and the recovery site, it is possible for an echo suppressor on long dial backup connections to block data transmission from the remote terminal, since it is operating in controlled carrier mode. Another disadvantage with this method is the requirement for dial backup connections from each remote terminal. Therefore, even for medium-sized multipoint networks, a large number of calls must be established and maintained, which requires a significant amount of time. A considerable amount of dial backup equipment and telephone lines will be required at the recovery site, and this approach can also affect local central office facilities at the recovery site. These factors should be investigated before this method is adopted.

The last approach involves running a new multipoint circuit to the recovery site and having drops at only critical terminal locations. As shown in Figure 10-7, the modem associated with the critical terminal cluster is switched from the existing to the new multipoint circuit. This method can provide a cost advantage when there is a concentration of critical terminals in a geographic area.

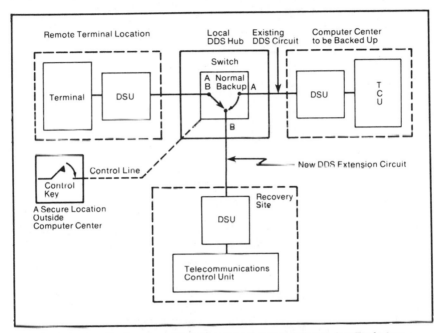

Figure 10-8. Backup for a DDS Circuit Using Circuit Extension Technique

AT&T's Dataphone® Digital Service (DDS) Circuits

Backup for DDS circuits can be provided by using the circuit extension technique and a tarrifed DDS switch. The operation is similar to that described for the analog circuits; a typical configuration is shown in Figure 10-8. An alternative is to provide an auxiliary modem and EIA switch, as shown in Figure 10-9, in which case 4-wire dial backup can be used to access the recovery site.

Locally Attached 3270

Many installations have local channel-attached IBM 327x equipment, which can present a real problem in backing up the facility. Several approaches can be considered, however. First, as shown in Figure 10-10, the

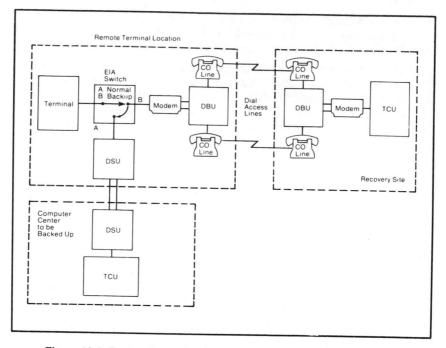

Figure 10-9. Backup for DDS Using Auxiliary Modem and Dial Backup

critical CRT terminals can be switched to a new teleprocessing-type controller; the controller can then interface to the recovery site over dial backup or private-line facilities. This approach generally requires software changes, which can be extensive.

Another alternative is to provide an additional local 327x controller and an interface minicomputer system that permits the local 327x controller to operate over communications links. A similar type of interface minicomputer is provided at the recovery site, and dial backup lines or private lines can link the two systems (as shown in Figure 10-11). The minicomputer systems translate the standard channel protocol to an HDLC-like protocol and back again and are available as standard offerings from several vendors. The local minicomputer at the recovery site typically can interface to a number of remote minicomputer units. Higher speeds can be achieved using an inverse multiplexing device; only minimal changes will be required within the teleprocessing software. With either approach, a response-time analysis should be made to determine the acceptable load on the links. Generally speaking, the direct-channel approach maintains a higher loading ratio because of the data transfer rate and efficiency in the protocols used.

Another solution to consider is designing the recovery site to permit the addition of local 327x equipment during a disaster. This presents logistical problems of floor space, relocation of personnel, files, telephones, and the like, all of which must be evaluated.

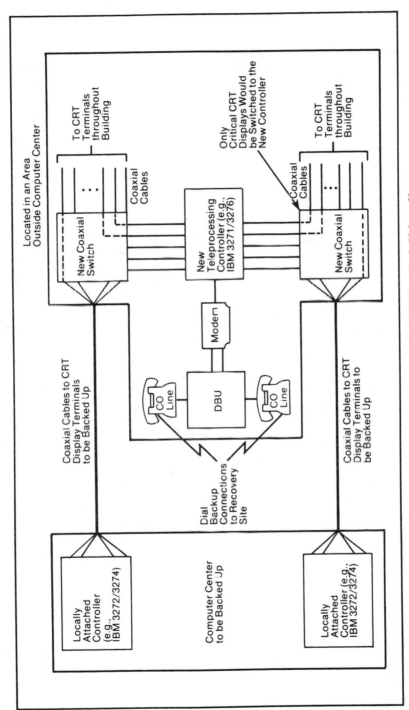

Figure 10-10. Backup for Locally Attached CRT Terminals Using a New Teleprocessing Controller

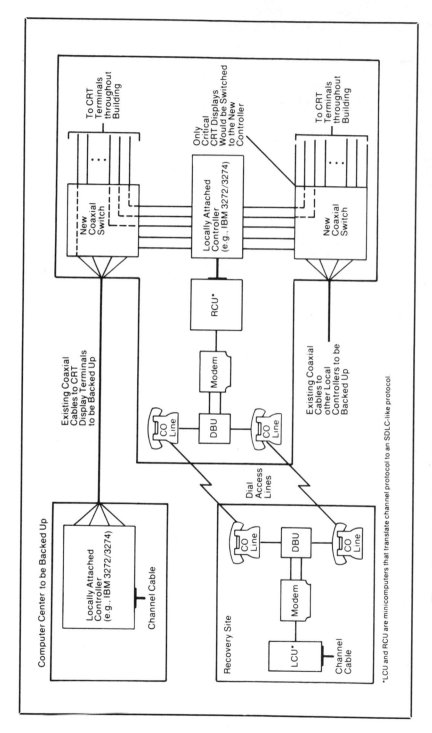

Figure 10-11. Backup for Locally Attached CRT Terminals Using an Interface Minicomputer

*LCU and RCU are minicomputers that translate channel protocol to an SDLC-like protocol.

High-Speed Remote Terminals

What can be done when it is necessary to back up a terminal or group of terminals that generally use a high-speed line at 19.2K, 50K, or 56K bits per second? First, as mentioned earlier, the critical work load should be evaluated to see if these bandwidths are required in a disaster situation. If the high data rate is still required, one of the following methods can be used. For 56K-bit-per-second DDS circuits, the circuit extension approach can be used. For analog wideband service, the costs are so prohibitive that it may be better to change the service to a digital one (if possible) that can be backed up using the circuit extension technique.

If the bandwidth requirements can be downgraded to 19.2K bits per second or less, an inverse multiplexor can be used to provide this speed on a dial backup facility. An inverse multiplexor (available from several vendors) divides the 19.2K bits per second into two 9.6K-bit-per-second channels, which can then be processed over dual dial backup facilities or two private-line facilities. A typical configuration is shown in Figure 10-12. If the full-rated bandwidth is required, at least one manufacturer offers an inverse multiplexor that can function at 50K and 56K bits per second, using up to six conventional 9.6K-bit-per-second channels.

Concentration Techniques

In many production networks, the terminals are geographically dispersed to such an extent that concentration techniques become economically unattractive. In the disaster backup network area, the problem is one of switching many lines, concentrated at the existing data center, to the recovery site. Switching does not necessarily mean user-initiated switching but simply that the switching must occur within the desired access time to the recovery site. For firms with a short access time, the switching function may require user initiation. For other firms (e.g., financial institutions), a store-and-forward message switch may be required to capture the data while the recovery site is being brought up.

As shown in Figure 10-13, using a simple statistical multiplexor to reduce bandwidth requirements to the recovery site can be economically justified for large backup networks if the recovery site will be used for a minimum of two to three years. The local multiplexor node would be located near the existing data center, and the circuits to be backed up could be interconnected to the multiplexor, using any of the techniques already discussed. As with any concentration approach, a careful analysis must be made regarding a failure at the local multiplexor node, since it carries the entire backup network.

Some production networks already use nodal architecture. In such cases, the most expedient way of backing up this type of network is to provide a node at the recovery site, with trunks provided to the nearest network node(s). Additional trunks can be established by dial backup or use of measured-time digital services on an as-required basis during a disaster. The ease and cost-effectiveness of accomplishing the network interconnection depends, to a large degree, on the architecture of the node. Disaster recovery requirements are thus additional design factors to consider when investigating nodal networks.

CONCLUSION

Evaluating the Methodologies

As part of the management team that will evaluate the methodologies for disaster recovery, the data communications manager will be asked to provide the estimated communications costs as well as the advantages and disadvantages of each approach. To perform this task, the manager should:

- List the critical applications to be supported. This information is crucial and frequently requires top management direction. Priorities should be based on how critical each application is to the firm and its sensitivity to the particular methodology. Certain applications, for example, may not function with the shell concept because they require specialized hardware that generally cannot be available in the required time unless special provisions are made.
- Determine the required recovery access time for the firm.
- Create a terminal/application matrix to identify the terminals corresponding to the critical applications.
- Determine which of these terminals are critical to the end user.
- Analyze the critical work load expected for each of these terminals, and create a transaction profile for each one.
- For batch terminals, perform a throughput analysis for the critical work load; for online systems, determine an acceptable response-time criterion per application in a disaster mode of operation.
- Analyze the use of shared communications facilities and alternate methods of information transfer to eliminate or avoid additional critical terminals.
- Complete a recovery backup network design.
- Obtain best vendor and carrier lead-time estimates for the backup network facilities.
- Identify the facilities whose lead times exceed the required access time: these must be installed beforehand.
- Based on the preceding steps, sketch a scenario or implementation plan on how the shell, second center, or vendor-supplied recovery site would be used.
- Determine budgetary costs, and address any outstanding problems.

It is recommended that these findings be used to compare alternative solutions by weighting each with its cost. For vendor- or cooperative-supplied recovery facilities, the following questions should be answered:

- Has the vendor or cooperative developed a reasonable plan to interface customer or member backup networks?

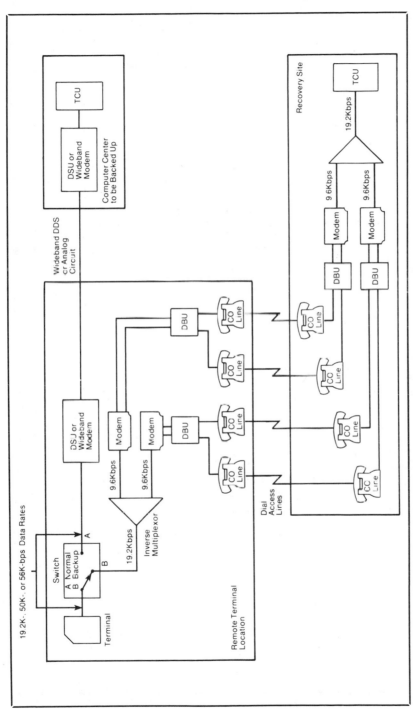

Figure 10-12. Backup for Wideband Terminals

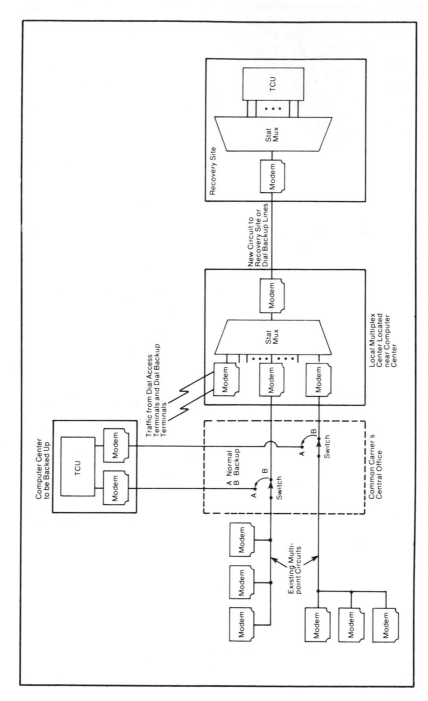

Figure 10-13. Backup Network Approach Using Concentration Techniques

- What cable entrance facilities are provided?
- How will the front-end requirements be met?
- What provision for equipment that must be in place has been made by the vendor or cooperative?
- Is there a flexible cost-sharing methodology available for specialized equipment or modems?
- Is testing available? If so, how often?
- Is documentation or a user manual available on how to use the recovery center's facilities?
- What facilities are provided at the recovery site in cases of extended outages?
- What support personnel and equipment are provided in the teleprocessing areas?
- What dial backup facilities, if any, are provided at the recovery facility?

The Planning Process

It is apparent that a great deal of the actual work will be performed during the evaluation stages. This work, together with ongoing inputs from the recovery team, will form the basis of the communications plan. The plan can be subdivided into strategic and implementation sections. The strategic section should state the goals, design objectives, and strategies relating to the backup network; the implementation section should describe the detailed steps in using the chosen recovery facility. A checklist of suggested major items to be included in the plan includes:
- A list of all assumptions, objectives, and strategies necessary for implementing the stated objectives
- A list of all tasks to be performed before, during, and after a disaster, including detailed timing charts (especially for the period of time immediately after a disaster is declared) as well as task dependencies, manpower estimates, and skill levels required
- A technical description of the backup network
- Primary and alternative personnel assignments and responsibilities
- An operational description of the backup network and an operational procedure for each terminal, explaining how to implement the backup network
- An overall scenario of how the recovery site will be used
- A list of all critical terminals, including location, telephone numbers, backup numbers, terminal type, manufacturer, characteristics, operator name, and so on
- A list of all vendor and carrier contacts who supply facilities in the backup network as well as their responsibilities
- Alternate sources of supply for equipment, facilities, and personnel
- Network diagrams and related documentation (e.g., software listings, equipment manuals, testing procedures, and operating procedures)

- A description of all circuit orders to be implemented in the event of a disaster and the common carrier contacts associated with each order
- Procedures for updating the plan and the ongoing support requirements

Making the Plan Work

It must be possible to modify the recovery plan through the normal organizational planning processes, and the management team concept should be used to keep this process up to date. As new applications are added, their criticality to the firm must be evaluated. The subset of critical terminals must be added to the terminal matrix and integrated into the recovery network. Facilities may have to be ordered, and if a vendor-supplied recovery service is used, the vendor must be aware of this additional requirement. It must be determined whether the recovery facility can provide backup for this new application. The organization is certainly affected, even if only through additional work that may require more resources. A permanent team of management representatives and a coordinator will probably be required to ensure that the firm is constantly protected.

A commitment to disaster planning, as demonstrated in this chapter, is no small task. Top management must be aware of the consequences of not planning as well as those of planning. The recovery network design can impose rather stringent design requirements not embodied in the production network. This chapter has also discussed some standard techniques that can be used to provide a recovery network at reasonable expense. Management should recognize that disaster planning is a continuous process that must be integrated into the firm's normal planning processes.

References

1. Stevens, C.A. "An Alternate Computer Site." *Journal of Information Management,* Fall 1980.
2. "When a Computer is Wiped Out." *Business Week,* November 20, 1978.
3. "An Evaluation of Data Processing Machine Room Loss and Selected Recovery Strategies." MISRC-WP-79-04. *Working Paper Series,* Management Information Systems Research Center. University of Minnesota, Minneapolis, June 1978.
4. Gaade, R.P.R. "Disaster Planning: Picking up the Pieces." *Datamation,* Vol. 26, No. 1, January 1980.
5. Lettieri, L. "Disaster Recovery: Picking up the Pieces." *Computer Decisions,* Vol. 11, No. 3, March 1979.
6. Miles, M. "Disaster Recovery Update." *Computer Decisions,* Vol. 12, No. 7, July 1980.
7. Stern, L, "Contingency Planning: Why? How and How Much?" *Datamation,* Vol. 20, No. 9, September 1974.
8. Trigaux, R. "Increasing DP Dependence Calls for Disaster Contingency Planning." *Bank Systems & Equipment,* July 1979.
9. Staller, Jack J., and Colling, David. "The Aftermath of a Computer Fire." *Fire Journal,* November 1977.